# How to
# Open &
# Operate
# a Financially
# Successful
# Notary
# Business

## With Companion CD-ROM

**Kristie Lorette and Mick Spillane**

# How to Open & Operate a Financially Successful Notary Business: With Companion CD-ROM

Copyright © 2011 by Atlantic Publishing Group, Inc.
1405 SW 6th Ave. • Ocala, Florida 34471 • 352-622-1825 • 352-622-1875–
Fax Website: www.atlantic-pub.com • E-mail: sales@atlantic-pub.com
SAN Number: 268-1250

Library of Congress Cataloging-in-Publication Data

Lorette, Kristie, 1975-
  How to open & operate a financially successful notary business : with companion CD-ROM / by Kristie Lorette.
     p. cm.
  Includes bibliographical references.
  ISBN-13: 978-1-60138-281-8 (alk. paper)
  ISBN-10: 1-60138-281-2 (alk. paper)
  1.  Notaries--United States--Popular works. 2.  New business enterprises--United States--Management.  I. Title.
  KF8797.L67 2010
  347.73'16--dc22
                         2010039591

PROJECT MANAGER: Marilee Griffin
BOOK PRODUCTION DESIGN: T.L. Price • design@tlpricefreelance.com
PROOFREADER : C&P Marse • bluemoon6749@bellsouth.net
FRONT COVER DESIGN: Meg Buchner • megadesn@mchsi.com
BACK COVER DESIGN: Jackie Miller • millerjackiej@gmail.com

Printed in the United States

Over the years, we have adopted a number of dogs from rescues and shelters. First there was Bear and after he passed, Ginger and Scout. Now, we have Kira, another rescue. They have brought immense joy and love not just into our lives, but into the lives of all who met them.

We want you to know a portion of the profits of this book will be donated in Bear, Ginger and Scout's memory to local animal shelters, parks, conservation organizations, and other individuals and nonprofit organizations in need of assistance.

**– Douglas & Sherri Brown,**
**President & Vice-President of Atlantic Publishing**

# Table of Contents

# Chapter 3: Becoming a Mobile Notary ... 39

# Chapter 4: Other Notary Services........... 45

# Chapter 5: Laws and Ethics......................55

# Part Two — Starting Your Notary Business...... 65

# Chapter 6: Getting Set Up.........67

# Chapter 7: Establishing an Office ........ 101

# Chapter 8: Create a Winning Business Plan ........................... 119

# Chapter 9: Managing Finances and the Business Budget ....................... 133

# Part Three — Expanding Your Business; Getting More Clients; Hiring Employees .................... 143

# Chapter 10: Marketing........................... 145

# Chapter 11: Developing an Online Presence ................................. 167

# Table of Contents

# Appendix C: Notary Website Resources ..................... 263

# Appendix D: Sample Business Plan ...... 265

# Introduction

The first thing that comes to mind when you think of a notary public may be a quiet, older woman who stamps documents for real estate transactions and car deals, but the fact is the notary public profession has been a profound and distinguished profession throughout U.S. history. Notaries have always had close ties to government agencies and the legal profession. The notary public profession is also the type of business that is easy to start and run as a home-based business, which is probably why you are reading this book in the first place. If you are interested in working from home, this book will act as your guide to starting a successful and profitable business as a notary public.

Almost everyone has dreamed of owning his or her own business. Often, these dreams are the result of dealing with difficult bosses, low pay, long hours, swing shifts, and other frustrations that come from working for someone else. In the safe confines of the imagination, the vision of owning a business is immensely satisfying: You are your own boss, you make your own decisions, and you do not have to answer to anyone else.

When you do something you enjoy, it does not feel like a burden as work sometimes does. An added bonus to being your own boss is the control of your own destiny by being as busy as you want and pulling in the income you desire.

One of the main benefits of launching a career as a notary is you do not need a college degree to become a successful, in-demand, and practicing notary agent. The notary business also makes a perfect career for a stay-at-home mom, retirees, those re-entering the work force, discharged military, or someone who has an entrepreneurial spirit because it is a career that offers endless possibilities for success and career advancement.

This book is one-of-a-kind in that it is your step-by-step guide to becoming a notary public and launching a successful and lucrative business. Included in the book are state-specific resources, industry terminology, and resources you can use to make the career and business launch seamless and within reach. The accompanying CD-ROM includes customizable and printable forms to use when planning each aspect of your business. Whether you are starting out as a notary or already established in the field, you will quickly learn each state's application process, training, and exam requirements to advance to the next level in your career and your business. This book delves into the state laws that preside over the practice of notaries, which is invaluable at any stage of your notary career.

After moving beyond the notary public career itself, the book then takes you to the heart of what it takes to launch and maintain a successful notary business. You will learn how to open your own notary business, work as a mobile signing agent, how to put your notary business on autopilot, and how to hire and manage employees. You will discover some of the types of industries a notary can provide services to and the fees charged for the notary services. The nuances of the notary business are explained and techniques on how to handle them are provided — from charging for traveling fees and handling no-shows and emergency notarization.

Not only does this book cover the basics of the notary business, but it also includes business forms, contracts, sample business plans, myriad checklists, day-to-day operation information, information on your notary stamp, and valuable time-saving tools that every business owner should have in his or her arsenal. You have embarked on your first step to becoming a notary public business owner by purchasing this book, which is a must have for a novice or a seasoned notary.

# PART ONE

# What You Need to Know About Becoming a Notary

CHAPTER 1 :

# Notary Basics

*T*he notary public profession dates back to ancient Rome, which makes it one of the oldest legal professions. Though the role of a notary may have altered somewhat from ancient to modern times, today governmental agencies and lawmakers recognize the role of the notary public as an important one.

Before getting too far ahead into the profession, it is beneficial first to understand the role of a notary in a legal transaction. A notary public is expected to assess the mental state of the signer of each legal document pertaining to a transaction and to carefully verify that the person who benefits from the document or is legally bound to sign the document is the person who signs it. Legal documents can range from those pertaining to a real estate transaction to professional license applications and forms. Because notaries confirm the legality of the signer of these transactions, the role is still vital, which means the notary profession will always have significance.

The National Notary Association, which is a professional organization established to meet the needs of the notary public profession, is constantly working to find new avenues where document and signature authentication is required. In the ever-changing world, where identity theft runs rampant, a notary public becomes an even more important protector and authenticator as a deterrent for identity crimes — giving the profession a pivotal role in immigration matters, anti-terrorism efforts, and the prevention of cybercrimes.

Many government and private agencies require notarized verification to ensure the validity of the documents processed on a daily basis. Security agencies, the armed forces, Social Security agencies, immigration, and motor vehicle departments are a few governmental agencies that use notaries public for identity verification and document authentication. Banks, insurance companies, financial institutions, mortgage companies, and Internet companies also need the services of notaries to secure documents.

Forgery and fraud are common methods of victimizing signers of documents. A notary public does not notarize a document without verifying the identity of the signer. A notary public is expected to explain the document to the signer as a means to assess the state of signer's mind and prevent him or her from signing under duress or under false representation. Some of the transactions notaries are required to authenticate include commercial transactions, real estate transactions, adoptions, affidavits, and powers of attorney.

By law, a notary cannot authenticate a document unless the signer is physically present and provides adequate proof of identity, such as a passport or driver's license. The notary public is an independent third-party professional witness to the transactions and does (and cannot) have a vested interest in the transaction. Thus, notarization adds a level of security and assurance that the document(s) involved in the transaction are genuine.

In the past, it was often cumbersome to find a notary. Even when you found a notary, you had to go to the notary, usually at a bank or legal office, and companies typically had to have a notary on staff. Modern times called for modern measures, and the mobile notary service was born in the 21st Century. With the convenience of having a notary come to you, a quick online search typically locates a local notary, and the possibility of hiring a notary at any time of day and any day of the week is possible.

As society becomes more time and cost sensitive, the concept of the mobile notary gains popularity. One reason is because notarizing documents can be a full-time job. Banks and legal offices may employ part-time notaries to handle notarizing documents that are part of daily business transactions or, at the very least, have one of its employees become a notary (depending on the volume of documents requiring notarization).

# Who Needs a Notary Public?

Banks, nursing homes, and hospitals are some of the many offices and organizations that require notary services. Car dealerships, insurance companies, title and mortgage companies, and real estate companies are other types of businesses that use notaries to notarize documents such as deeds, wills, contracts, eviction notices, affidavits, and bankruptcy applications.

# Why Become a Notary?

A career as a notary public allows you to make your own schedule (either part-time or full-time work) and choose which clients and projects which to accept. Being your own boss as a notary public affords you flexibility, which can allow you to supplement your current income or create a full-time income. The notary profession is an important one in the legal community, as they perform various. various duties such as:

▶ Administering oaths and declarations

▶ Aiding as a witness to and authenticating documents

▶ Performing marriages (in some jurisdictions)

Being a notary public affords you the flexibility to choose whom you work for, where you work, and even when you work. Whether you are looking for a part-time job, a full-time business opportunity, or a way to supplement your income by doing freelance work, the notary profession can be the perfect career for you.

# What Is Notary Document Signing?

Many documents for legal and other purposes require notarization. Notarization affirms the parties involved are willing and able participants, which verifies the validity of the documents. When something has been notarized, it does not necessarily mean the document is considered a legal document; it means the parties signing are agreeing on a certain issue. This issue can be anything from a loan to submitting an application. The process of notarizing requires a few quick and easy steps, which is established as a simple formula that most notaries are required to use in their business.

When documents are notarized, the document requiring notarization must be on hand and a government-issued identification for each signing party must be presented. The notary uses a state-issued notary stamp and seal to complete the transaction. A notary is not allowed to sign a document if he or she believes that one of the parties is entering into the contract unwillingly or if the notary suspects fraudulent activity.

Many different legal situations require notarized documents, such as court documents, affidavits, loans, marriage licenses, and divorce. There are typically three steps involved in notarizing a document:

1. Screening the signer

2. Making a journal entry

3. Completing a notarial certificate

Basic types of certifications include:

▶ Acknowledgment certificate (a certificate signed by an authorized official)

▶ Jurat (the notary certifies having viewed the signing of a document and administering an oath/affirmation where the signer declares the document to be truthful.)

▶ Copy certification (the notary certifies a deed, certificate, record, or document to be a factual and accurate copy of the original)

## Notary Associations

Joining a notary association provides networking opportunities to mingle with and learn from fellow notaries. Associations typically provide seminars, workshops, and training sessions to keep up-to-date with the constantly changing notary laws. Often, these groups and associations offer members benefits including:

▶ A hotline that supports notaries with any notarial issue that may arise

▶ Newsletters that provide up-to-date information about notarial issues that directly affect you and your job duties

▶ Discounts on notary supplies

▶ Insurance options, such as personal identity theft insurance

- ▶ Access to a wide variety of professional information and resources

- ▶ Personal listing in the association's notary locator

- ▶ Association-issued credit cards

- ▶ Local classes and professional conferences

*You can find a listing and contact information for the various notary associations in existence in Appendix C.*

Now you have basic knowledge of the need and importance for the notary profession, it is time to learn about becoming a notary public.

---

## CASE STUDY: THE PASSION FOR BECOMING A NOTARY

Deborah Glomb
Deborah Glomb Realty, Inc.
3850 SE 58th Ave. Ocala, FL 34480
Office number: 352-624-3151
BUYFLA1@aol.com

For Deborah Glomb, it was destiny. It was in her genes, her blood to become a notary. Glomb's mother and stepfather had a notary business; she was bitten by the notary bug as a precocious young girl and sought to have her own notary business. Through the guidance of her mother and stepfather, she was able to realize her dream. Glomb was afforded the luxury of being able to take the time to establish herself independently from her family and was able to define herself more clearly. She realized in the beginning of her career that whether or not you stay in the family business or start your own, you will be a happier person for making the decision honestly.

As her parents brought the next generation of their family into the notary business, it was still an innocent time. The business was run out of her mother's home, but they were one of the first to realize the service of being a mobile notary. They would travel to people's homes, to their jobs, and even nursing homes and hospitals.

Glomb saw the big picture; she was thinking outside the box. She expanded into the real estate field. Her business is a corporation with two other notaries, three realtors, and a receptionist. Her real estate company notarizes property owner documents, wills, school papers, and loan and refinance documents. It also offers property management and rentals. One of the notaries at her corporation specializes in weddings. To make things run more smoothly in her business, she has incorporated the notary and real estate business into one business instead of two separate businesses, which makes things a lot easier for day-to-day work life.

Glomb is a people person, a trait she learned from being under the guidance of her parent's notary business. She enjoys meeting the needs of her clients. Of course, working flexible hours is bonus, especially when she has a husband, three grown children, and six grandchildren; she defines her success in balancing her business and family life.

Glomb starts each day at 6:30 a.m. with coffee and a sensible breakfast. She feeds her dogs and cats, tends to her garden, and then leaves for the office by 9 a.m. She takes care of e-mails as soon as she gets to the office, returns calls, and sets up appointments. She plans property inspections for a half a day and completes about five inspections in the afternoon.

The one thing Deborah would like to remind all notaries of, her basic piece of advice, "They are not bankers, lenders, or attorneys; never give advice!"

# CHAPTER 2 :
# Becoming a Notary

Once you commit to becoming a notary, the next step is to turn to resources such as the American Society of Notaries (ASN), which is the first national nonprofit association for notaries public in the United States as well as the leader in education, support, and supplies for the notary in America (**www.asnnotary.org**).

Because each state has its own licensing requirements for notaries (minimum age requirements, passing a state-issued exam, the length of a notary's practicing commission, and residency requirements), you can uncover the requirements for your state and the duties your state permits notaries to perform.

General guidelines and regulations for notaries in various states:

▸ In Delaware, South Carolina, Vermont, West Virginia, and Georgia, an attorney must be present or otherwise involved in the closing of real estate transactions.

▸ In Indiana and Maryland, notaries must possess title insurance license for all property closings.

▶ In Massachusetts, an attorney must be present or otherwise involved in the closing of real estate transactions. Notaries who are working with a lender can notarize a document in direct combination with closing of the employer's loans.

▶ Nebraska and North Carolina impart notary fee limitations. In addition, ancillary fees, such as courier fees, may not be charged.

▶ Nevada imparts notary fee limitations, including hourly travel fees based upon time of day or night.

▶ In Texas, home equity lines of credit must be signed and closed in the office of the mortgage lender, attorney, or title company.

▶ In Utah, notaries can notarize and obtain signatures for title escrow settlement documents. For any other duties, a notary must obtain an escrow license.

▶ In Virginia, notaries are prohibited from conducting real estate property signings without an escrow license.

The Internet and your local library are other rich sources of information on the notary profession. Here are some helpful websites to review:

▶ **www.nationalnotary.org**: National Notary Association provides advice and expert insight on how to become a notary (for example, training classes, conferences, news, and resources).

▶ **www.notaryofamerica.com**: Notary of America contains a compilation of common questions and information on becoming a notary.

Although each state is different in terms of licensing notaries, similarities exist as well. The typical step-by-step process to become a licensed notary (*See Appendix B for further information on state requirements.*):

**Step 1: Application.** Obtain, complete, and submit the notary application to secretary of state's office for the state where you will perform notary duties.

You must include the application fee payment (about $60.00, although the fee will vary from state to state) Typical questions on the application include:

- Name
- Gender
- Social Security number
- Date of birth
- Mailing address
- Current occupation
- Name and address of your current employer
- Home and employment telephone numbers

The application may also include questions such as:

- Are you at least 18 years old?
- Have you ever been convicted of a felony? (The application requires you to explain the offenses if you answer yes.)
- Can you read, write, and understand English?

**Step 2: Research your state regulations.** As stated previously, regulations vary per state. Some of the more rigorous application processes require fingerprinting and a background check because you will work closely with the legal and government communities. However, these scrupulous requirements are necessary only after the applicant passes the state-issued notary exam; conversely, some states do the fingerprinting process when the notary exam is administered.

**Step 3: Prepare for the test.** Several options are available to prepare applicants for their upcoming test, including books, online test prep classes, test prep study guides offered by your state, and even classes given by working notaries at adult education centers or at community colleges.

- ◆ Once your application has been approved, which on average takes a few weeks, you may then register for your state's notary exam. More often than not, there is another fee for the exam, although it is much smaller than the initial application fee. (The average state's fee is $15.00 for the exam.)

- ◆ The basic test most states give is in the multiple-choice format. Applicants generally have an hour to complete approximately 40 questions. The exam is pass or fail, and the applicant must answer at least 70 percent of the questions correctly to pass. Results are mailed to the applicant, usually within a few weeks of the exam.

- ◆ Once you have passed the exam, mail back your pre-approved application with your test results to the appropriate county or state office, or go to the county clerk's office to file an oath.

**Step 4: Take an oath of office.** Upon successfully passing your notary exam, the final step to becoming a notary is to take an oath, frequently given by the county clerk, though sometimes the oath is directly incorporated into the application itself. Below is an example of how Pennsylvania's oath appears:

| Notary: | Do you solemnly swear that the statements contained in this affidavit are true to the best of your knowledge and belief? |
|---|---|
| Affiant: | I do. |
| Notary: | Do you solemnly swear that the testimony that you are about to give will be the truth, the whole truth, and nothing but the truth. |
| Affiant: | I do. |

*Notary Public's Oath of Office*

*Commonwealth of Pennsylvania (_____ ) SS: County of _____*
*I, Joe Q. Notary, having been duly appointed and commissioned a Notary Public in and for the Commonwealth of Pennsylvania, do solemnly swear (or affirm) that I will support, obey and defend the Constitution of the United States and the Constitution of this Commonwealth and that I will discharge the duties of my office with fidelity.*

Even after you take your oath, you are not quite ready to launch your career because you need a few supplies first: a notary stamp seal/embosser and a notary journal.

# Tools of the Trade: Notary Supplies

As with any job, certain supplies are required to perform notary duties. Notaries use a notary stamp and a notary journal, which are personal to the notary and under no circumstance can be shared with anyone else because they are the notary's professional records.

A journal of notarial acts, or your notary journal, is of vital importance because you must have a permanent record of every notarial transaction you perform. Its sole purpose is to serve as evidence in the case of lost or altered documentation. Your notary journal should be a bound book with page numbers and blank numbered entries that you fill out in chronological order when you begin notarizing. The page numbers and binding prevent fraudulent insertions and deletions of entries.

Every blank journal entry is identical and self-explanatory (see Figure 2-1). For each notarial act you perform, there should be a corresponding entry in your journal. There should also be a separate entry allotted per signer. You should make sure to fill out each entry in your journal prior to notarizing a document to ensure the signer does not walk away before the transaction is complete.

**FIG.2-1.EXAMPLE OF A BLANK ENTRY IN A NOTARY JOURNAL**

| | | #14 |
|---|---|---|
| Printed Name of Signer | Signer's Signature | Time: _____ |
| _____ | _____ | Date Notarized: _____ |
| Signer's Address: | City      State | Zip      Phone |
| _____ | _____  _____ | _____  _____ |
| Identification by: __ ID card | Issued by: _____ | ID # _____ |
| __ Personal Knowledge | Type of ID: _____ | Ex. Date: _____ |
| __ Credible Witness(es) | Date of Birth: _____ |  |

• • • • • • • • • • • • • • • • • • • • • • • • • • • • • • • • • • • • •

Type of Notarial Act: __ Verbal Ceremony Performed          __ Other (describe)

__ Oath/Affirmation          __ Acknowledgement

Fee: $                    RIGHT THUMBPRINT OF

Travel: $                 SIGNER HERE

• • • • • • • • • • • • • • • • • • • • • • • • • • • • • • • • • • • • •

| Type of Document | Date of Document | Witnesses | Other Signers |
|---|---|---|---|
| _____ | _____ | __Y  __N | __Y  __N |
| Witness: Printed Name | Address/Phone | Witness Signature | |
| _____ | _____ | _____ | |

Comments/Additional Info:          If Notarization Failed/Refused, Give Reason:

__ Insufficient ID          __ Signer Confused

__ Other (Explain) _____

The information for each entry will vary, based on the notarial act you are completing. Be consistent with information to ensure each entry is completed in full and before the signer leaves.

Due to the increasing problems of identity theft, some notaries request a thumbprint as a means to detect fraud. This is an extra safeguard and not required. Use your own discretion with each notarial act for which you are hired.

The information contained within your journal tends to be sensitive legal documents. Therefore, proper safeguards should be in place to protect your journal. It should be kept in a safe and secure location, such as a safe deposit box.

It is a legal requirement to keep your notary journal current and up-to-date (check with your state for its requirements). To be on the safe side, keep your journal for at least seven years after your notary commission has expired, revoked, or you decide to resign.

Your notary stamp/seal and embosser is the next vital piece of equipment you will need once you pass your exam. Your notary stamp is a stamp with your name, the state and county in which you are commissioned, and the expiration date of your commission. Your commission can vary, but usually it expires five years from the date in which it was issued. You usually will apply your stamp directly to the document you are notarizing to prove it as valid. Figure 2-2 is an example:

**FIGURE 2-2.**

The stipulations regarding documentation for your stamp seal/embosser vary. You may need the following when ordering your stamp: original commission certificate, certificate of authorization, letter of passing, certificate of appointment, letter or appointment, or new law letter (contingent upon state of license). Before ordering your stamp, it is best to check with your state's notary commission or notary association for the most up-to-date requirements. You can also check the website for the American Association of Notaries, **www.notarypublicstamps.com**, to obtain the necessary supplies based on your state's requirements.

It is important to take good care of your stamp, which means keeping it clean to provide clear, legible, and a legal stamped impression. Following are some tips to keep your stamp clean:

▸ When not in use, keep your stamp covered.

▸ To clean your stamp, apply a piece of clear tape over the impression of the stamp and remove.

▸ Do a sample stamp on a scrap of paper before officially stamping a document.

When you order your custom-made embossing tool, it imparts an embossed notary seal on a document. The information included is your name, county, and state commission (Figure 2-3). A simple Internet search will yield numerous notary supply stores where you can purchase this item. Sites including **www.xstamperonline.com**, **www.notarypublicstamps.com**, and **www.notarysupplyshop.com** provide a wide variety of notary supplies.

**FIG. 2-3. EMBOSSED NOTARY SEAL**

# Notary Supplies Checklist

It does not matter if you are a freelance notary, employed by a business, working from home, or have an office outside of the home. The following are basic office supplies to get you started and help you become successful:

▸ A dedicated work space

▸ Landline phone with voice-mail service

▸ Computer

▸ Fax

▶ Printer

▶ Letterhead

▶ Business cards

▶ Notary journal

▶ Notary seal stamp/embosser

▶ Black pens (all notarial documentation must be signed in black ink)

▶ Notary certificates

▶ Error and omissions insurance (if applicable)

▶ Receipt book

▶ Stapler

▶ Thumbprint pad

▶ Jurat forms

Once you have your notary business supplies organized, it is just as important to stay organized.

# Staying Organized

You studied and passed the exam; you have taken your oath; and now you have all of your tools for the trade. Starting your notary business can be stressful, but keeping things organized will make life easier. Staying organized with the everyday tasks associated with running your business, as well as keeping long-term goals in mind, brings ease to administering tasks. Some ways to stay organized include:

▶ If you decide to work from home, keep your work area separate from the rest of your home. It is essential to your new professional and personal life to maintain a specific work area in your home. You cannot leave your work problems at an external space anymore, and keeping a separate space helps draw the line between personal time and work time. Keep everything work related neatly arranged in your workspace. When you need to do something for work, head to your work-designated area; this will allow you to give your full attention to each project.

▶ Maintain a secure area in your home office for all of your notary supplies, so you can find them when you need to use them.

▶ Maintain a work calendar just for work to help you organize appointments and work-related projects.

▶ Create a filing system, such as:

- Establish projects by categories: for example, real estate, mortgages, emergency services, and weddings.

- Create an index system based alphabetically or numerically.

- Make folders for current projects and have separate folders for future projects.

When it comes time to deal with the paperwork associated with being a notary public, assess every notarial document and consider the following:

- Does this need to be saved or discarded? Can I research it on the Internet (e.g., a policy change)? Be sure to read the document thoroughly before disposing of it and make notes of any pertinent information that you need for your files.

- If the file is important for your records, file it immediately rather than put it off for later.

Once you have met all the basic requirements and purchased the equipment to become a successful notary, it is time for you to explore some of the options available to you and for your business. One of the most popular services notaries offer today is a mobile notary service. The next chapter is devoted to exploring what a mobile notary does, so you can decide if it is a service you are interested in adding to your new business venture.

## CASE STUDY: COMMITMENT TO BEING A NOTARY

Myra Anne Healey
JP-Online Services
Weare, NH 03281
www.JPOnlineNH.com

Myra Anne Healey is a notary in New Hampshire and has been in the business for 28 years. She became a notary because she was self-employed with her ex-husband, and they found the need to have a notary in their office. After her divorce, Healey was interested in continuing self-employment, so she decided to put her notary certification to good use. Now, she offers mobile notary services, works with loan closings, and handles field services.

Healey feels it is much too easy to become a notary in New Hampshire, and she believes there should be more training for prospective notaries. When she received her notary certification, there were few qualifications and no formal training. The only requirements were that you were 18 years of age, a registered voter, and did not have a criminal background. The training consisted of receiving a pamphlet with your certificate.

One of the most important things to know while practicing as a notary is the law that applies in your state, says Healey. She also recommends that you keep accurate records of every notarization, whether it is required or not in your state. It is important to keep your record book, notary stamp, and seal in a safe place. You should always act with confidentiality when performing your duties as a notary. It is also important to remember to never notarize a document if the person does not have proper identification or has expired identification.

Being self-employed definitely has its benefits when it comes to flexibility. Healey makes her own hours and answers only to herself. Her typical hours vary depending on what she has scheduled for that day. If she has no jobs scheduled for mobile services, then she is usually in her office catching up on paperwork or marketing her business via the Internet or telephone. If she must work on the road, she tries to schedule appointments for the morning or afternoon so that she can be back by the later part of the afternoon to catch up on daily paperwork, invoicing, and answering e-mails (which typically reaches a couple hundred per day). On these days, she tries to get out of the office by 9 p.m.

Healey feels that marketing your business is of the utmost importance when self-employed. In the beginning, she advertised to mortgage companies, title companies, and anyone else that she thought could use her services. Now, her marketing efforts include advertisements, a website, membership in different groups and associations, and continuously searching for new business and new ways of generating business. She is part of several organizations where her services are offered to people who are looking for notaries.

For Healey, the most rewarding aspects of her career are having the ability to meet new people and knowing that her services are much appreciated. There are some difficult aspects of the job, however. It can be difficult when she comes across a document that is confusing but does feel that after all her years as a notary, there really is nothing she has not seen. She enjoys knowing that she is responsible for her own business and that she only has herself to blame if she does not take on jobs. Healey says that sometimes, or most times, the hours are long; you have to wear many hats in the same day, and you have to be flexible and able to multitask.

Healey says that the best advice she can give to anyone looking to start his or her own notary business is to do your best, be consistent, and do not try to rip anyone off. She says that you should make sure to give the same exceptional customer service at all times, even if you have underbid the job. Make sure to stick to all commitments.

# CHAPTER 3 :
# Becoming a Mobile Notary

*T*oday, mobile notaries play an even bigger role in the business environment as people's lives become more hectic. Being a mobile notary is similar to being a notary public; however, as the name suggests, you are traveling to businesses, people's homes, hospitals, and other locations rather than having them come to you. You can either start out as a mobile notary or expand your service offering to include mobile services.

Before you decide to extend the scope of your business to include mobile notary services, first consider finances, logistics, and emotional factors involved in being ready and on call when a client calls you.

Expanding your notary service does not guarantee profit. In fact, you may be creating more work and expenses by offering mobile services. Working as a mobile notary could mean more overhead: travel, gas, and being on call.

## Mobile Notary: The Right Career Move?

Once you have passed the exam and obtained your license, you need to establish your business network. Fortunately, most companies and business organizations prefer a notary on call rather than on the payroll, which gives you the freedom to earn as much as you want (or can). The fee for a notary on call can range from $25 to $200 according to the type of services you are performing for the client. In order to cover some of the additional expenses, such as travel costs, mobile notary fees are higher than the fees charged when clients come to the notary.

## When is a mobile notary called to action?

In our ever-shrinking global economy, we never know when the need may arise for the notarization of a document. It can be rather tedious to go all the way to the bank or to visit the neighborhood notary. Sometimes documents need to be notarized, and other notary offices are not open because it is after business hours or a holiday. If you decide to become a mobile notary, these clients turn to you for their after-hour and holiday notarization needs.

## What services do mobile notaries offer?

Most mobile notary businesses offer several main services. Many mobile notaries offer the service of loan signing, which is useful if a loan needs to be signed in a place that does not already supply a notary. This could be because the loan is exchanged between two friends who only need the notary for legal purposes or in a pinch when a company's typical notary cannot meet. Mobile notaries are also used in the mortgage industry, loan closings, adoption papers, and wills and estates situations that may fall outside of normal business hours.

With the services offered by a mobile notary service, it is possible to get something notarized right on the spot. Not only is this good for customers, but it is also good for the notary. It is likely that notaries are able to bring in more business and make more money on their own than they ever would as a part of a larger company or being in a stationary location.

## *The pros and cons of a mobile notary service*

When considering starting a mobile notary business or adding mobile notary services to your new business venture, it is important to look both at the pros and cons to going on the road.

The most notable benefit of a mobile notary business is it opens up a new realm of business because being able to sign on the go generates more business opportunities. Another benefit of being a mobile notary is it is not necessary to have an office, which can cut down costs and make it easier to turn a profit. Of course, if you employ others, then it still may be necessary to have an office. Another benefit to having a mobile business is that documents can be notarized much faster. Being able to move from appointment to appointment eliminates downtime while waiting for clients to arrive.

Though starting a mobile notary business can seem easy at first, there are still some concerns. The main concern is that with a mobile business comes more work. Most mobile notary businesses are open for business more hours than stationary notaries. People may expect a notary to come to them at any hour of the day, any time of the week, and any time of the year, which can be draining on you. Another con to a mobile notary business is the expense of travel is much higher than for stationary businesses. When traveling from place to place, expenses can add up quickly, especially if gas prices increase. You also have to worry about safety concerns because you may be entering clients' homes.

Most states only allow notaries to charge their clients a certain amount of money per transaction (generally up to $200, depending on the service) but there are ways of bringing in more income when you are the one traveling to a client. As is the case with many other businesses, you can charge for traveling expenses. In the case of using a mobile notary, the customer does not wish to come to your home or office; consequently, they pay you for the convenience of you coming to them.

There are an equal number of pros and cons for starting a mobile notary business. If you would rather drive around to a business, a mobile notary service could be perfect. Conversely, if you would rather have people come to you, then a mobile notary service may not be the right option for you.

Aside from the mobile notary services, you can get involved in several other aspects of the notary business, so the next chapter explores other ways you can generate business as a notary.

# CASE STUDY: MOBILE NOTARY SERVICE

Marc Greco
Founder of Nationwide Notary Network
www.n3notary.net
info@n3notary.net
800-455-1146

Nationwide Notary Network provides mobile notary services in every city throughout the United States. With notaries available 24 hours a day, seven days a week, and same-day appointments, N3, as the business is called, typically offers clients notary services within two hours. N3 is a networking site that works with more than 3,500 independent notaries around the country. N3 matches the client's service needs with a locally contracted notary in the client's area.

Marc Greco, founder of N3, has been a notary for four years and started the company in 2003 as an S corporation. To become a notary in Oregon, Greco had to take a 20-question, open-book test. The fee for becoming a notary in Oregon at that time was $20. He decided to enter into the notary industry after a friend told him about the mobile notary work that he was doing. Greco, looking for a change of pace, jumped on the opportunity.

Greco believes that the best notaries are reliable, honest, know what their responsibilities are, and what they are not. In his business, the aspect he enjoys most is working with the community of notaries, hearing their stories, and being able to help people. When asked what challenges notaries face, he said, "I think one of the biggest challenges a notary faces is knowing when to refuse a notarization. This could mean having to tell your employer that you cannot notarize a document because it was not signed in the notary's presence or informing the family members of a terminal patient with days or less to live that the notarization cannot take place because the patient cannot communicate with the notary in a meaningful way."

A typical day for a N3 representative includes sales, notary management, customer support issues, scheduling notary contractors, recruiting, staff and cash management, system development, and strategic planning. He believes that next to sales, marketing is the most important thing that his business does. The business uses Internet advertising, Yellow Pages advertising, and direct mail campaigns as their main means of marketing their services. N3 is a member of the Better Business Bureau and the National Notary Association. Greco believes these affiliations are important because being a member of the BBB lends credibility to the business, and being a member of the NNA keeps the business up-to-date on issues in the notary industry.

Greco says that the most enjoyable aspect of being a business owner is that it allows him the ability to create and to take an idea and make it into something people will enjoy and come back to. When asked to offer advice for someone considering this profession, he said, "If being a notary public is something you are looking to do to make a full-time income, then learn everything you can about how to operate a profitable business, set goals, and be realistic about what you can achieve as a notary public. Keep in mind that the secretary of state will determine the rate you can charge per notarization, and in some states, this can be as much as $10 or as little as 50 cents." Other advice he offers is to "build relationships with other notaries and service providers that have a continuing need for a notary public, join a notary association such as the National Notary Association, and learn about the opportunities that exist for notaries in your area."

# Other Notary Services

$\mathcal{A}$s you become comfortable in your career as a notary public, you may discover your role overlaps with other job functions in banks, law offices, and mailing and shipping stores. In some cases, notaries may have experience as paralegals. With a combination of paralegal experience, banking, other law-related experience, and your experience as a notary, it opens the door to expanding your notary services. This chapter explores some business opportunities notaries use to add revenue streams.

## Becoming a Notary Signing Agent

A notary signing agent is a notary public who has been trained and tested in the knowledge of presenting documents used in real estate refinance loan transactions. It is normal for notary signing agents to take an examination on their knowledge of the correct procedures of loan document signing procedures and the notary public laws of their state. You can become a certified notary signing agent by taking an online, self-study course through the National Notary Association website, **www.nationalnotary.org/NSAcertification**.

As a notary signing agent, you tend to work on contract; you are, in effect, a freelancer working as needed for title or mortgage companies. You will provide this service to clients in the comfort and privacy of their own homes or offices. The pay can be excellent; moreover, you can dictate your own schedule and accept or decline jobs as you see fit.

There are different options for a notary signing agent. For example, a mortgage notary signing agent is brought in as a notary public who specializes in real estate loan transactions — specifically the closing of real estate loan transactions. Loans are closed by correspondence — meaning by mail — so the lenders depend on notary signing agents to complete the signing and notarizing of real estate documents with the clients and then return the completed and executed documents to the lender. For further information on this service, visit the website of the National Notary Association.

# Working With a Signing Company

The main function of a loan signing company is to help close loans by securing low rates and offering a fast approval process. An example of a signing company is America's Best Closers (**www.americasbestclosers.com**).

Now that it is possible to apply for and get approved for a loan over the Internet, the loan process has become faster for borrowers; consequently, lenders may have an overflow of borrowers and need of qualified, dependable notary signing agents to help meet these needs.

A notary signing agent ensures the loan documents are understood by the client, that required signatures are obtained on the documents, and then notarizes the signatures where necessary.

The difference between a notary and a signing agency is that the agency goes a step further by helping clients get their loans approved over the phone or electronically. The signing company acts like an attorney by smoothing out the legalities of signing any paperwork involved. Keep in mind a signing company does not offer legal advice, but some of the roles a signing company may play include:

▶ **Facilitation:** A signing company reviews client documents and guides clients on finalizing the papers according to the law. The company ensures the loan papers are signed and notarized accordingly.

▶ **Expediting the process:** The signing company not only notarizes the signature of the borrower, but also ensures the papers are in order so there are no issues when the papers are submitted to the lender. With the relationship the signing company has with the lender, these companies typically are able to negotiate faster processing times for the client.

▶ **Field inspections:** The signing company also may perform field inspections to provide the necessary and accurate data and other information to assist the lender in making a decision. Field inspection work may include visiting the property the mortgage is being made on, taking photographs, and submitting a written report to the lender on the condition of the property.

The signing company offers services that simplify the lending process and reduce expenses and any inconveniences of the loan or mortgage process. A signing company works with insurance, mortgage, bond, loan, reverse mortgage, private and commercial investment companies, and individuals. A signing company is an ally to both the creditor and the borrower because the signing company facilitates the transaction.

## The future of signing companies

As a nation that seeks instant gratification, a loan signing company fills this need by offering a one-stop shopping for closing loans. Due to this convenience, working with a signing company can increase the revenue of your notary business, and consequently your income.

The primary reasons for having a signing company in addition to your notary business are to enhance your income and to become a well-known presence in your field. You can link up with title and mortgage companies that are eager to outsource their notary signing and witnessing business. Especially when mortgage and title companies are trying to keep overhead expenses down by reducing employees, businesses look to refer business to a notary business outside of the company. It is also viable for a notary to close loans for three or four different lenders in a single day.

The job of a notary signing agent is not an easy one. As is the case with any job, work as a notary signing agent has its drawbacks. Being successful requires you to establish yourself and possibly work long or additional hours because you typically will be on call.

# Adding Real Estate Agents into the Mix

Because the housing and mortgage industry is a cyclical business, it can cause ebb and flow in the business of a notary that works in these industries. The buying or selling of homes is timeless, so working within these industries can be a lucrative venture.

Working in the real estate field is still one of the best ways for a notary to ensure more business and increased income. Working with a real estate company or with specific real estate agents is an excellent way to increase profits and business by notarizing documents involved with real estate and mortgage transactions. With the experience and training as a notary, you will be an asset to a real estate agency when you understand real estate and mortgage loan documents. When working with real estate agents, you are helping the agents' clients accurately complete and return the documents for processing to the title or escrow company. The service you are providing is a crucial one because it moves the real estate and mortgage loan transaction to completion. As a notary, you may be required to travel to a client's home or office or conduct the notary services at the office of the real estate agent or title or escrow company's office.

This service can reduce the borrower's settlement costs. It also frees up time for the closing agency, which increases the volume of loan closings an agency can undertake.

If you choose to work in the real estate field, you will be handling more documents; therefore, you are required to pass a state exam to obtain a certificate or commission. Even though you have to pass an exam, most of the time you will be dealing with the phones, customer service, administrative duties, notarizing documents, and networking your services.

# Title Searching

Another way to add additional income is to add title searches to your menu of services. A title search is conducted on a piece of real estate to verify ownership and to identify any liens or claims on the property.

The most common reasons for a title search involve a property being bought, sold, or refinanced. In a mortgage transaction, the mortgage company wants to know who has an ownership interest in the property and what other liens may exist on the property. A clear title, one without liens, is typically required before the transfer of ownership, such as transferring ownership from the seller to the buyer, can take place.

## Using PACER

A title search protects people from others who would claim that a piece of property is theirs when it is not. If you are hired to complete a title search or decide to add this service to your notary business, it will most likely take place at the county courthouse where property records are located. However, you might be able to do your title research online. To find out if your courthouse has a website, complete the following steps:

- ❏ Go to **www.findlaw.com/11stategov.**
- ❏ Scroll down to locate your state.
- ❏ On the next page, click "Courts."
- ❏ From this link, you can find the courts in your state.

To search court records you need a user ID and password, which is issued by PACER (Public Access Court Electronic Records). Most bankruptcy courts across the United States currently are available online for record searching. You will only need a PACER login and ID, which are free.

Once you have received your PACER login and ID, do the following:

- ❏ Login to **www.pacer.psc.uscourts.gov.**
- ❏ Click on "Links to PACER Websites."
- ❏ Choose "Appeals," "Bankruptcy," or "District" courts.
- ❏ Choose the court you want to search.
- ❏ Enter your PACER login and password to access the court.

For the notary doing title searches, PACER is an invaluable tool. If you incorporate title searching into your notary business, it might be a tool you use daily; therefore, you should familiarize yourself with PACER to use it properly and efficiently.

# Virtual Bankruptcy Assistant Service

Another sound business expansion for the notary signing agent is providing a virtual bankruptcy assistant (VBA) service. A virtual bankruptcy assistant helps people who are filing for bankruptcy by using knowledge or expertise to help the client file accurately. The service provides the bankruptcy filing forms, helps the client complete the forms, and faxes the forms to the attorney handling the bankruptcy proceedings.

A virtual bankruptcy assistant is used in a number of law offices, because it eliminates the need for employees. Virtual bankruptcy assistants work autonomously, so this service is ideal for the notary who works independently and wants flexible hours. It is typically more attractive to the client who is going through bankruptcy to require your services as a virtual bankruptcy assistant instead of an attorney because it is less expensive than an attorney, is not a face-to-face transaction, and is less embarrassing to the client. A number of people cannot afford attorneys and are looking around for solace in somebody who can help, at least in regard to paperwork, making this trying time in their lives a little bit easier.

This field requires extra training. The National Association of Virtual Bankruptcy Assistants, **www.navba.org**, is the only organization to offer the VBA Certification exam. The test will evaluate your understanding and capability of preparing a bankruptcy petition. It is worth it to expand your small business as a notary signing agent. Learning to prepare bankruptcy petitions takes place under the direct tutelage of a consumer bankruptcy attorney. For more tips on how to prepare for the exam, visit **www.vbacertification.com/prepare.html**.

# Get Secular: Branching into Weddings

A public notary in Florida, Maine, and South Carolina has the special privilege of being able to perform wedding ceremonies. A notary can administer oaths and solemnize a marriage. Many couples opt for the nontraditional route and use the services of a notary public to officiate their marriage. This makes it easy for notaries to expand into the wedding business.

If you are a notary in one of these states and decide to pursue this service, there are some things to take into consideration. First, a wedding is a scripted event, so you should have some wedding ceremony vows you can work from for the wedding. People are counting on you to make this one of the most beautiful days of their lives. Performing wedding ceremonies tends to take some practice. You can find a sample wedding script on the Florida Notary Association, Inc., website, **https://www.flnotary.com/become-a-notary/important-information/190-2**, or consult a priest or minister for advice.

## Becoming a marriage-based notary

Especially for popular destination wedding destinations in the states that allow a notary to perform wedding ceremonies and notarize the marriage license, it may be viable to focus your notary services on weddings. Adding wedding services your business and can increase your income.

Most notaries set wedding rates by the services they provide. In Florida, you can charge $20 per wedding, according to the Florida Notary website, **www.floridanotary.org/become-a-notary.html**. Someone driving to a wedding to notarize the marriage license would not charge as much as someone who officiates the ceremony.

If marriage-based notary services interest you, there are certain things you need to do to focus your business on just weddings and marriages. The first part is deciding everything you plan to do for weddings and marriages. What services do you want to offer in addition to the basic notarization? Once you decide what to offer, line up venues or vendors so when someone uses your services, everything is ready.

Advertising is a large part of becoming a marriage-based notary. Make a website that discusses your willingness to be a marriage-based notary and officiate. You can also place ads in bridal magazines, the Yellow Pages, and pamphlets. Advertising your services to wedding event professionals can be a great way to increase the volume of your business. For example, join efforts with a wedding planner so she can refer clients to you that are need of someone to officiate their wedding ceremony. *More about advertising and creating a website will be discussed in Chapters 10 and 11.*

# CHAPTER 5:
# Laws and Ethics

*W*hen practicing as a notary public, legal issues may come up. Whenever you are dealing with legal issues, agreements, and contracts, it is important to educate yourself. Consequently, for a notary, there are occurrences you want to try to avoid. One of the most important legal concerns that a notary must be aware of is the signing of documents by the wrong parties. It is important for the notary to be aware of exactly who the people are who wish to sign the papers. Almost every state mandates photo identification so the notary can tell if they are the ones who are supposed to be signing the document. If someone other than the person who is supposed to sign the document signs it, and the notary did not ask for identification, the notary could be subject to legal actions. The notary could be regarded as being a party involved in identity theft, according to the North Dakota State Government website, **www.nd.gov/sos/notaryserv/pdf/nn-122003.pdf**.

Another issue notaries face is fraud. If a notary uses the information that he or she has access to for illegal gain, it is against the law. It is necessary for notaries to be careful to keep accurate records to avoid this.

Further delicate issues may arise for a notary. A notary is not authorized to give legal advice to anyone. If someone claims they received legal advice from a notary, the notary's license can be revoked. Notaries also are not allowed to create any legal documents or appear as a legal representative for someone in a legal case. If a notary lends his or her equipment — stamp or embossing tool — to someone else, it is also a cause for revocation of a notary license, as this act is prohibited by law. It also voids the contract or document notarized because it was not executed legally. This can cause the parties involved in the transaction to suffer damages, which the notary may be liable for paying.

# Gramm-Leach-Bliley Act (GLBA) and Its Effect on NSAs

In 1999, Congress passed the Gramm-Leach-Bliley Act (GLBA), which is intended to protect the privacy of consumers. Because of this act, the mortgage industry requires compliance training and background screenings for anyone directly involved in the lending process. Therefore, notary signing agents, because they have access to the borrowers' sensitive financial information, are also required to follow the strict privacy laws enacted by the GLBA. These restrictions and laws are introduced in the notary signing agent training course.

# IRS Regulations for a Notary Public Business

As with any business that generates income, issues arise between owners of notary public businesses and the Internal Revenue Service (IRS).

The net income of a notary public is normally subject to federal income tax. Even though it is considered self-employment, income from this type of business venture is not subject to any self-employment tax according to Section 1402(c)(1) of the Internal Revenue Code and Regulations Section 1.1402 (c)-2(b). However, if the notary public has another business and is declared as a self-employed individual, he or she is obliged to pay the self-employment tax based on the net income from the other business. This is why most financial and business advisers suggest that when you open a notary public business, you separate your business and personal income and expenses from each other.

You may want to meet and discuss the tax and financial implications of establishing a notary business with a tax adviser and/or the IRS before opening for business.

# Understanding Copyrights and Trademarks

## Intellectual property

Intellectual property refers to inventions, literary works, and symbols, names, images, and designs used in commerce. Intellectual property is becoming one of the most important resources to a business. Therefore, it is important to have all materials and documents copyrighted and notarized. In our ever-shrinking global society where everything is a mouse click away, having all signatures notarized can be a simple and economical way to thwart an expensive nightmare. Notaries public work with copyrighted materials and trademarks; therefore, they should have a clear understanding of these laws. Other forms under the umbrella of intellectual property items are trademarks, patents, and design rights.

## Copyright

Copyright is the private, legal right of an author of a creative, intellectual property to control the copying of his or her work. These laws protect the author of intellectual property and grant the right to control who can copy or derive work from that original work. A copyright is considered a form of personal or business property. As a rule, a work must meet certain criteria to establish its originality before a copyright will be issued for it. Below is a list of claimable works that are protected by copyright, according to the United States Copyright Office (**www.copyright.gov**):

- ▶ Literary works
- ▶ Musical works
- ▶ Dramatic works
- ▶ Pantomimes and choreographic works
- ▶ Pictorial, graphic, and sculptural works
- ▶ Motion pictures and other audiovisual works
- ▶ Sound recordings
- ▶ Architectural works

Originality is an odd term, in this case, because two different works may be strikingly similar, yet original. Copyright laws provide protection to what are considered "works of the mind," which cover not only music but also literary, film, photography, and all other forms of artistic expression. The determining factor is whether each author or artist published his or her work and the similarities between that work and another person's work are coincidental, or whether the works were copied. The only time the original author or artist is not considered for originality is if the work was hired out, or "work for hire." In that situation, unless agreed upon by the employer and person hired to complete the work, the copyright is not shared between the two parties. One of them will have full ownership of all rights to the copyright.

These laws that offer protection do have their pros and cons, specifically in the terms of the powers that control who expresses the medium, and who can use it. Ownership of a copyright allows the owner to authorize other parties to make use of the work. The copyright owner usually requests some sort of financial licensing arrangements or may refuse authorization to use the copyrighted work if they feel it is for an inappropriate use or will devalue the work. U.S. law permits "fair use" of intellectual property for educational or nonprofit purposes. Unauthorized use or infringement of copyrighted material may be a civil or criminal matter because it is unauthorized use.

The copyright holder has certain rights, which can be enforced in civil and criminal courts, including the right to reproduction and distribution of the item that was copyrighted. Other rights included with the copyright are the right to adapt the work (such as to change it over to stage, film, or musical work); the right to public performances or displays; broadcast rights (transmitting the material through motion pictures, sound recordings, and performances); the right to import/export (publication distribution and copyright transfers); and the ability to sell the copyright to another party.

The copyright can only be exempted with the permission of the current holder, or owner, of the copyright.

## Universal Copyright Convention

The Universal Copyright Convention (UCC) was established in Geneva, Switzerland, in 1952 to establish formal procedures such as registration, a minimum copyright period of the lifetime of the author plus 25 years, and that all copyrighted works carry the UCC symbol © plus the year of the first publication.

In 1952, the United States recognized the UCC and gave formal recognition to the copyright works of other member states, including Great Britain. The United States did not make addendums to its copyright procedures until March 1, 1989.

## *Trademark*

A trademark is considered intellectual property and commonly applies to a distinguishing logo, design, words, name, symbol, or phrase. It may also consist of any combination of these.

A trademark is used to distinguish the exclusive source of a particular product or service and frequently is identified by a brand logo or name. It can be identified by the inclusion of the standard trademark symbol ™. Companies often use the trademark to differentiate their products and product names from similar products competing companies offer.

The trademark holds up in a court of law only if the offending party has attempted to pass its product off as an original product from the trademark holder. Otherwise, the logo, name, and symbol still can be used by the broad public.

When applying for a trademark, the holder must identify which products, services, name, letters, shapes, packaging, labels, devices, or signatures fall under the umbrella of that trademark. In addition, any color combinations that significantly identify that trademark must be listed on the application. There must be some form of representation graphically and that graphic must appear on any product or service that is registered with it. For example, the FedEx® logo identifies itself from other companies, such as UPS® and USPS.

There are other more specialized forms of trademark, including collective trademarks (which indicate membership in an organization, such as American Bar Association or Rotary International®), defensive trademarks (which serve as protection for well-known trademarks), certification marks, and generic trademarks. Generic trademarks are used to describe a wide range of products that fall into a certain category. A few generic trademarks are well known, such as Dumpster, Cellophane, and Thermos®.

# Copyright and Trademark Issues Pertaining to Your Notary Business

When you begin your notary business, the issues of greatest concern to you are issues dealing with property.

One area of property identification that may present problems is the authentication of intellectual property. Corporations market products and services using product names that have been trademarked, which requires authentication with regard to the date. When someone uses a particular intellectual invention without permission and infringes on a copyright, the date of creation of the invention is vital. In the case of trademarks, the date of use of the trademark is important because when another business uses the same or a deceptively similar name on a subsequent date for another product, the prior date will be the evidence presented to court to prevent usage of the name.

Throughout your notary business, customers may ask you to notarize the date of copyright or trademark documents in the presence of witnesses. But your notary seal may mean little in the eyes of the law. On the contrary, Rule 902(8) of the Federal Rules of Evidence in a U.S. court states the following:

> *Extrinsic evidence of authenticity as a condition precedent to admissibility is not required with respect to the following: Acknowledged documents. Documents accompanied by a certificate of acknowledgment executed in the manner provided by law by a notary public or other officer authorized by law to take acknowledgments.*

What does this legalese mean? It means that when a person's signature has been notarized, courts waive the legal requirement of verifying authentication of the contract and that alone can save you a great deal of time and money in the courts.

Your notary seal does not guarantee intellectual property rights and cannot be used as a substitute for trademark or copyright registration. Copyrights should be filed and registered with the U.S. Copyright Office in Washington, D.C. Patents and trademarks should be registered with the U.S. Patents and Trademarks Office in Washington, D.C.

# Ethics of a Notary

To ensure the highest levels of professionalism and conduct, the National Notary Association has implemented a comprehensive code of ethics that all notaries should abide by. The following is the Ten Guiding Principles taken from The Notary Public Code of Professional Responsibility:

**THE NOTARY PUBLIC CODE OF PROFESSIONAL RESPONSIBILITY**

# TEN GUIDING PRINCIPLES

1. The notary shall, as a government officer and public servant, serve all of the public in an honest, fair, and unbiased manner.

2. The notary shall act as an impartial witness and not profit or gain from any document or transaction requiring a notarial act, apart from the fee allowed by statute.

3. The notary shall require the presence of each signer and oath taker in order to carefully screen each for identity and willingness and to observe that each appears aware of the significance of the transaction requiring a notarial act.

4. The notary shall not execute a false or incomplete certificate, nor be involved with any document or transaction that the notary believes is false, deceptive, or fraudulent.

5. The notary shall give precedence to the rules of law over the dictates or expectations of any person or entity.

6. The notary shall act as a ministerial officer and not provide unauthorized advice or services.

7. The notary shall affix a seal on every notarized document and not allow this universally recognized symbol of office to be used by another or in an endorsement or promotion.

8. The notary shall record every notarial act in a bound journal or other secure recording device and safeguard it as an important public record.

9. The notary shall respect the privacy of each signer and not divulge or use personal or proprietary information disclosed during execution of a notarial act for other than an official purpose.

10. The notary shall seek instruction on notarization and keep current on the laws, practices, and requirements of the notarial office.

It should be the notary's highest priority always to perform notary duties impartially and with confidentiality. If there is some conflict and you are unable to be both impartial and maintain your signer's confidentiality, you should refer the signer to another notary who can perform the transaction. Holding yourself responsible for maintaining the ethics of a notary is a key factor in becoming a successful professional.

## Notary pledge of ethics

The following is the Notary Signing Agent Pledge of Ethical Practice prepared by the National Notary Association. This pledge is to be presented to each borrower at the beginning of each closing so that he or she understands the role of their notary signing agent.

> *I am not an attorney and therefore, by law, I cannot explain or interpret the contents of any documents for you, instruct you on how to complete a document, or direct you on the advisability of signing a particular document. By doing so, I would be engaging in the unauthorized practice of law and could face legal penalties that include the possibility of incarceration. Any important questions about your document should be addressed to the lender, title company, or an attorney.*

# PART TWO

# Starting Your Notary Business

# CHAPTER 6:
# Getting Set Up

*N*ow that you have a firm understanding of the role of a notary and all of the services a notary can provide, it is time to evaluate your ability to be a business owner on top of being a notary. The question you have to ask yourself is: Are you ready to start your own business? Starting your business means you take complete responsibility for the outcome; it is a serious venture not to be taken lightly. At first, you will have to cut corners, market yourself, and track down new clients; you typically have to work long and grueling hours to start and build a successful notary business.

However, in the notary business, the odds are on your side because this profession grows every day. On another positive note, the startup costs for a notary business tend to be lower than those of many other types of businesses. Approach starting your notary business with a realistic viewpoint, and make sure that you have what it takes to be your own boss.

When you are staring your new business venture, it may be advantageous to become a notary signing agent (NSA), which was explained in Chapter 4. By gaining experience in the real estate and mortgage business, you are adding to your skills set as a notary, which can grow your customer base and increase the amount of money you can earn. For example, the typical notary public will make a few dollars signing documents. An NSA, however, can make anywhere from $100 to $300 for every signing he or she is contracted to do.

# Ready for Self-Employment

The idea of running your business and being your own boss does seem exciting and fun at first. Creating your schedule and setting your own deadlines is an enviable lifestyle. You can become a self-employed professional running a small service business from home or from your business's new office. As a business owner, to guarantee a profit you must run your business just as any other business managers would run a business. It is essential to develop good business habits right from the beginning.

Being self-employed does not have to be difficult. The first step is to develop a plan of attack. If you still have your day job, attempt being a notary part time or as a second job until you can build a client base. You at least will have a steady income to manage bills and living expenses. Moreover, you will be bringing in extra income from being a notary. Do not overwhelm yourself at first with juggling two careers. Ease into this new business venture, because it will be an adjustment. Once you have gained a foothold in the world of being a notary, you can quit your previous job and focus on your new business as a notary public.

The simple fact is major changes will take place in your life once you have established your new business as a notary. Focusing on new responsibilities requires you to make adjustments. With your previous career, you already had a self-defined role of who you were, as well as a steady paycheck. With your new business venture, you will have to depend on yourself to make a profit.

## CASE STUDY: FULL-TIME NOTARY LIFESTYLE

Natasha Kennedy
Long and Forrester Realtors, Inc.
Chantilly, VA
Office: 202-363-1800
Direct: 571-235-8545
www.KennedyRealtor.com

Natasha Kennedy had long established herself in the real estate field. She specializes in investment property, new construction, and works with first-time home buyers. This past year has found her branching out into the area of the notary public.

Kennedy saw a niche market and took advantage of that situation. As a realtor, her clients always need something notarized, and she noticed that it has been a problem to find a notary, especially a mobile notary. She saw that many of her clients are elderly with limited mobility and cannot drive; thus, she added the service of a mobile notary. Kennedy had a clear understanding of how vital the undertaking of a mortgage signing agent is to the successful closing and funding of the real estate transaction. She has used her expertise in real estate, which gives her knowledge in presenting documents used in real estate refinance loan transactions.

Kennedy studied to be a notary signing agent and completed an examination on her knowledge of the correct loan document signing procedures and the notary public laws of her state.

Being a full-time notary has given her that "enviable lifestyle" — the lifestyle that allows flexibility in her schedule. This is important to Natasha because it gives her time to be at home with her children. This flexibility also gives her extra time to market her business, which she does through the Internet and a neighborhood newsletter. The newsletter is another creative way to reach out to clients and find new clients.

Kennedy's secrets to being a successful notary and real estate agent: staying focused, responding promptly, and being available 24/7.

# Business Basics

Becoming a small business owner is rewarding and challenging. Simply put, the more you know about how a business works, the more likely your business will run successfully. Though the idea of operating your own business sounds appealing, you must deal with some harsh realities. Discover some of the top myths and truths of being a business owner to gain a more realistic view of what running a business entails.

## Myth 1: Being your own boss is simple.

Everyone assumes that owning your business means you are leading a cavalier lifestyle. This is not usually the case. Although it is true you are your own boss, it also means you are responsible for every aspect of your business, both good and bad. Because you are the owner, manager, and CEO, everything rests on your shoulders. Even if you have expanded your business and hired the best people possible to assist you with this venture, mistakes will happen, and it is your responsibility to fix them.

Also, bear in mind that you are ultimately the one who must deal with a dissatisfied customer. The customer is always right; they are the ones who pay your bills. You have to learn how to deal with clients because they are the key to your business success.

## Myth 2: As the owner, your work schedule will be more flexible.

One of the biggest business myths is that a business owner works during operational hours only (and as the boss you get to only show up when you want to), normally nine to five, Monday through Friday. Though you will have some degree of flexibility, you ultimately are tied to deadlines. If work has to get done after hours, over the weekend, or when you are sick, the burden of these tasks falls upon your shoulders. It may be nice to set your hours, but you are still the sole person responsible for meeting deadlines, emergencies, and adapting to nontraditional client scheduling.

## Myth 3: As owner you will work fewer hours.

The myth of working fewer hours while making more money may be the goal, but you have to be realistic. Everyone dreams of being able to work less and earn more money. Unfortunately, even for business owners, this is not a reality. The truth is, you may have the potential to exceed breaking even, but you will also need to work hard to get to that point. In the beginning, do not be surprised if you have to work 12-hour days, seven days a week. This work schedule is typical and not at all the exception to the rule.

Every entrepreneur knows the majority of small businesses do not make it past their first year of operation; this is a fact. According to the U.S. Small Business Administration, more than 50 percent of small businesses fail in the first five years. One of the reasons they fail is because the owner was not willing and able to give everything he or she needed to give to make the business work. Insufficient funds, lack of capital, and poor location also contribute to business demise, according to Michael Ames, author of *Small Business Management*.

If you truly want to run a business with staying power, you need to be willing to work hard for as long as it takes, even at the expense of vacations and family activities. You must make your business the first priority in your life until it becomes well established. Only then can you consider more flexible hours and recreational activities.

# Creating Your Schedule

One of the myths of setting your hours is you are more relaxed and at ease. Sure, you have time to run to the bank, the dry cleaners, and do all of your errands on your own time without asking for permission. However, working on your own does have its downside — scheduling.

Due to your newfound freedom of working for yourself, it can be hard to motivate yourself and be disciplined. The most important thing to remember is never miss a deadline and never forget an appointment. If you miss appointments, chances are, the client will not trust you or give you repeat business.

Discipline should always be the focus when starting a new business schedule. Creating your work schedule takes discipline and excellent time management. It is easy to say that you will work from nine to five, but what happens if you get sidetracked running those errands, or worse, decide to rent a movie or go to a long lunch instead? If you are not willing to adhere to the schedule you set for yourself, then there is no point in setting a schedule.

## Your schedule and your life

This is your business and your life, so it is up to you to decide what type of schedule you would like to create. Yes, you do have choices in the matter. You can have a set schedule or a more flexible schedule that you determine each day depending on how much work you have. When creating your schedule, it is important to maintain some type of routine because this will result in a more productive workday. Regardless of the type of schedule you set, you still have deadlines, appointments, paperwork, and all the other things that one has to do to maintain a business.

Here is an example of a daily schedule:

| 9:00 a.m. - 9:30 a.m. | Rise and shine. |
|---|---|
| 9:30 a.m. - 10:30 a.m. | Breakfast and check e-mail. During the workday, focus on work-related e-mail. Now is not the time for catching up on gossip. |
| 10:30 a.m. - 11:30 a.m. | Return phone calls; make appointments; do follow-up with clients. |
| 11:30 a.m. - 12:30 p.m. | Take care of any errands that need to be completed. |
| 12:30 p.m. - 1:00 p.m. | Lunch |
| 1:00 p.m. - 2:30 p.m. | Complete outstanding paperwork, and bring notary journal up to date. |
| 2:30 p.m. – 3:30 p.m. | Check e-mail, return phone calls, and follow up with clients you were unable to contact earlier in the day. |
| 3:30 p.m. - 4:30 p.m. | Make sure all client account management is current. Schedule appointments for meeting with clients and attending to notary signings. |
| 4:30 p.m. - 5:00 p.m. | Plan for any notary signing appointments for that evening or the next day. |
| 5:00 p.m. - 6:00 p.m. | Take care of invoices or follow up with outstanding invoices. |

# Scheduling Your Work

Every day may be different running your notary business, but there will be tasks you must complete regardless of what is on your daily schedule. For example, checking your e-mail, returning and making calls, and completing invoices all need to be attended to each day. These may be tedious tasks, but they are important to your business. Make time for them first thing in the morning so you may allot large chunks of time for your notary projects.

## *Plan for the unforeseen*

Life is full of little surprises; consequently, you really cannot create a schedule that details every minute of your day. Your day will be full of interruptions: e-mail, phone calls, faxes, and more. Therefore, do not burden yourself with over-scheduling. Your day will be so hectic you will not get anything done. It will take some time to settle into your routine, and once you become more comfortable, you will learn how to manage your time properly. For the moment, leave some pauses in your schedule that will allow you time to do the dishes, cook, and attend to the unexpected.

## *Flextime*

As previously discussed, when starting your business, you are not always going to be working nine to five. Freelancers and many people with their own business prefer flextime, which can accommodate their lives, their families, and outside obligations, because life can be unpredictable.

Flextime means you are working hours that are suitable to your lifestyle. With a business, you may have to be more resourceful when creating your schedule. Flextime allows your schedule to cater to other obligations and interests in your life. The idea of flextime is to allow balance in personal and professional life.

# Reviewing Your Schedule

Now that you have created your schedule and settled into a routine, each week you should take time to evaluate your week. Consider the following when doing your evaluations:

- ▸ Were all work-related tasks completed in a timely and efficient manner?
- ▸ Is there a way to add more or less to each weekly schedule?

▶ How was your personal or flex time affected?

Now, you should be able to determine if the schedule is working for you. Is there a different way to manage different tasks? Again, you do have choices with your schedule; see what works for you because it will give you greater peace of mind when it comes to your work and personal life.

Once you have decided that you are ready to take on the challenge of being the owner of a business, it is time to consider how to legally structure your business.

# Determine the Legal Structure of Your Business

Deciding which legal structure you would like to build your business under will be the backbone of your operation. The legal structure of your business sets the platform for your everyday operations and influences the way you proceed with financial, tax, and legal issues — just to name a few. It will even play a part in how you name your company, because you will be adding Inc., Co., LLC, and such at the end of the name to specify what type of company you are. It will dictate what type of documents need to be filed with the different governmental agencies, and how much and what type of documentation you will need to make accessible for public scrutiny. Also, it will define how you operate your business. To assist in determining how you want to operate your business, following is a description of the different legal structures, along with a sample of documents you may need to file with state and federal agencies, depending on where you live.

# Business Entity Chart

| Legal entity | Sole proprietorship | Partnership | LLC | Corporation |
|---|---|---|---|---|
| Costs involved | Local fees assessed for registering business; generally between $25 and $100 | Local fees assessed for registering business; generally between $25 and $100 | Filing fees for articles of incorporation; generally between $100 and $800, depending on the state | Varies with each state, can range from $100 to $500 |
| Number of owners | One | Two or more | One or more | One or more; must designate directors and officers |
| Paperwork | Local licenses and registrations; assumed name registration | Partnership agreement | Articles of organization; operating agreement | Articles of incorporation to be filed with state; quarterly and annual report requirements; annual meeting reports |
| Tax implications | Owner is responsible for all personal and business taxes | Business income passes through to partners and is taxed at the individual level only | Business income passes through to owners and is taxed at the individual level only | Corporation is taxed as a legal entity; income earned from business is taxed at individual level |
| Liability issues | Owner is personally liable for all financial and legal transactions | Partners are personally liable for all financial and legal transactions, including those of the other partners | Owners are protected from liability; company carries all liability regarding financial and legal transactions | Owners are protected from liability; company carries all liability regarding financial and legal transactions |

# Becoming a Small Business

A small business is a company with fewer than 500 employees. You will be joining more than 26 million other small businesses in the United States, according to the Small Business Administration. Small companies make up 99.7 percent of *all* employer firms in the country and contribute more than 44 percent of the total U.S. private payroll. More than half are home-based. Franchises make up 2 percent of these small businesses.

Of those 26 million small U.S. businesses, the SBA states that 649,700 new companies first opened for business in 2006. During the same period, 564,900 of the 26 million total closed shop. However, ⅔ of newly opened companies remain in business after two years and 44 percent after four years. The odds are with startups. Just keep in mind that virtually every company that survives does so because the owners are working hard and care about their company.

# Sole Proprietor

Sole proprietorship is the most prevalent type of legal structure adopted by startup or small businesses, and it is the easiest to put into operation. It is a type of business is owned and operated by one individual and is not set up as any kind of corporation. Therefore, you will have absolute control of all operations. Under a sole proprietorship, you own 100 percent of the business, its assets, and its liabilities. Some of the disadvantages are that you are wholly responsible for securing all monetary backing, and you are ultimately responsible for any legal actions against your business. However, it has some great advantages, such as being relatively inexpensive to set up, and with the exception of a couple of extra tax forms, there is no requirement to file complicated tax returns in addition to your own. Also, as a sole proprietor, you can operate under your own name or you can choose to conduct business under a fictitious name. Most business owners who start small begin their operations as sole proprietors.

Some examples of the types of businesses that set up shop as a sole proprietor include consultants, executive notaries, and even wedding planners. Because a notary public can run a business alone, it is a viable option for establishing a notary public business as well.

# General Partnership

A partnership is almost as easy to establish as a sole proprietorship, with a few exceptions. In a partnership, all profits and losses are shared among the partners. A profit is the positive gain after expenses are subtracted, while a loss occurs when a company's expenses exceed revenues. In a partnership, not all partners necessarily have equal ownership of the business. Normally, the extent of financial contributions invested in the business determines the percentage of each partner's ownership. The percentage of ownerships also relates to the amount of revenue due to the partner and the amount of financial and legal liabilities the partner is responsible for. One key difference between a partnership and a sole proprietorship is that the business does not cease to exist with the death of a partner. Under such circumstances, the deceased partner's share can either be taken over by a new partner or an existing partner. In either case, the business is able to continue without much disruption.

Although not all entrepreneurs benefit from turning their sole proprietorship businesses into partnerships, some thrive when incorporating partners into the business. In such instances, the business benefits significantly from the knowledge and expertise each partner contributes toward the overall operation of the business. As your business grows, it may be advantageous for you to come together in a partnership with someone who has knowledge and experience that complements your own to contribute toward the expansion of the business. Sometimes, as a sole proprietorship grows, the needs of the company outgrow the knowledge and capabilities of the single owner, requiring the input of someone who has the knowledge and experience necessary to take the company to its next level. This is where a partnership typically comes into play.

When establishing a partnership, it is in the best interest of all partners involved to have an attorney develop a partnership agreement. Partnership agreements are legal documents that normally include information such as the name and purpose of the partnership, its legal address, how long the partnership is intended to last, and the names of the partners. It also addresses each partner's contribution, both professionally and financially, and how profits and losses will be distributed. A partnership agreement also needs to disclose how changes in the organization will be addressed, such as death of a partner, the addition of a new partner, or the selling of one partner's interest to another individual. The agreement must ultimately address how the assets and liabilities will be distributed should the partnership dissolve.

# Limited Liability Company

A limited liability company (LLC), often erroneously referred to as limited liability corporation, is a hybrid of a corporation and a partnership. An LLC encompasses features found in the legal structure of corporations and partnerships, which allows the owners — called members in the case of an LLC — to enjoy the same liability protection of a corporation and the record keeping flexibility of a partnership, such as not having to keep meeting minutes. In an LLC, the members are not personally liable for the debts incurred for and by the company, and profits can be distributed as deemed appropriate by its members. In addition, all expenses, losses, and profits of the company flow through the business to each member, who ultimately would pay either business taxes or personal taxes — and not both on the same income.

An LLC type of business organization would be most appropriate for a business that is not quite large enough to warrant assuming the expenses incurred in becoming a corporation or being responsible for the record keeping involved in operating as such. Yet, the extent of its operations requires a better legal and financial shelter for its members.

Regulations and procedures affecting the formation of LLCs differ from state to state, and they can be found on the Internet in your state's "corporations" section of the secretary of state office website. Two main documents are normally filed when establishing an LLC. One is an Operating Agreement, which addresses issues such as the management and structure of the business, the distribution of profit and loss, the voting method of members, and how changes in the organizational structure will be handled. The Operating Agreement is not required by every state.

Articles of Organization, however, are required by every state, and the required form generally is available for download from your state's website. The purpose of the Articles of Organization is to establish your business legally by registering with your state. It must contain, at a minimum, the following information:

- The limited liability company's name and the address of the principal place of business
- The purpose of the LLC
- The name and address of the LLC's registered agent (the person who is authorized to physically accept delivery of legal documents for the company)
- The name of the manager or managing members of the company
- An effective date for the company and signature

Articles of Organization for an LLC filed in the state of Florida will look something like this:

**ARTICLE I — Name**

The name and purpose of the Limited Liability Company is:

Fictitious Name International Trading Company, LLC
Purpose: To conduct…

**ARTICLE II — Address**

The mailing and street address of the main office of the Limited Liability Company is:

**Street Address:**   1234 International Trade Drive
                      Beautiful City, FL 33003

**Mailing Address:**  P.O. Box 1235
                      Beautiful City, FL 33003

**ARTICLE III — Registered Agent, Registered Office, and Registered Agent's Signature**

The name and the Florida street address of the registered agent are:

John Doe
5678 New Company Lane
Beautiful City, FL 33003

*After being appointed the duty of registered agent and agreeing to carry out this service for the above mentioned Limited Liability Company at the location specified in this certificate, I hereby agree to take on the assignment of registered agent and will perform in this capacity. I further agree to adhere to all statutes and provisions associated with the proper and complete performance of my tasks, and I am knowledgeable with and agree to the conditions of my position as a registered agent as outlined in Chapter 608, Florida Statutes.*

_____

Registered agent's signature

**ARTICLE IV — Manager(s) or Managing Member(s)**

| **Title** | **Name & Address** |
| --- | --- |
| **"MGR" = Manager** | |
| **"MGRM" = Managing Member** | |
| MGR | Jane Doe |
| | 234 Manager Street |
| | Beautiful City, FL 33003 |
| MGRM | Jim Unknown |
| | 789 Managing Member Drive |
| | Beautiful City, FL 33003 |

**ARTICLE V — Effective Date**

The effective date of this Florida Limited Liability Company shall be January 1, 2009.

**REQUIRED SIGNATURE:**

_____

Signature of a member or an authorized representative of a member

# Corporation

Corporations are the most formal type of all the legal business structures discussed so far. A corporation is the most common form of business organization and is chartered by a state under its laws. A corporation can be established as public or private. A public corporation is owned by its shareholders (also known as stockholders) and is public because anyone can buy stocks in the company through public stock exchanges. The shares or stocks owned by shareholders represent a financial interest in the company. Not all corporations start up as corporations, selling shares in the open market. Corporations may start as individually owned businesses that grow to the point where selling its stocks in the open market is the most financially feasible business move for the organization. However, openly trading your company's shares diminishes your control over it by spreading the decision making to stockholders or shareholders and a board of directors. Some of the most familiar household names, like the Tupperware® Corporation and The Sports Authority®, Inc., are public corporations.

A private corporation is owned and managed by a few individuals who are normally involved in the day-to-day decision making and operations of the company. If you own a relatively small business, but still wish to run it as a corporation, a private corporation legal structure would be the most beneficial form for you as a business owner because it allows you to stay closely involved in the operation and management. Even as your business grows, you can continue to operate as a private corporation. There are no rules for having to change over to a public corporation once your business reaches a certain size. The key is in the retention of your ability to closely manage and operate the corporation. For instance, some of the large companies that also happen to be private corporations include Domino's Pizza®, L.L. Bean®, and Mary Kay® cosmetics.

Whether private or public, a corporation a legal entity capable of entering into binding contracts and being held directly liable in any legal issues. Its finances are not directly tied to any personal finances, and taxes are addressed separately from its owners. These are only some of the many advantages to operating your business in the form of a corporation. However, forming a corporation is no easy task, and not all business operations lend themselves to this type of setup. The process can be lengthy and put a strain on your budget due to all the legwork and legal paperwork involved. In addition to the startup costs, there are additional ongoing maintenance costs, as well as legal and financial reporting requirements not found in partnerships or sole proprietorships.

To legally establish your corporation, it must be registered with the state in which the business is created by filing Articles of Incorporation. Filing fees, information to be included, and its actual format vary from state to state. However, some of the information most commonly required by states is listed as follows:

- Name of the corporation
- Address of the registered office
- Purpose of the corporation
- Duration of the corporation
- Number of shares the corporation will issue
- Responsibilities of the board of directors
- Status of the shareholders, such as quantity of shares and responsibilities
- Stipulation for the dissolution of the corporation
- Names of the incorporator(s) of the organization
- Statement attesting to the accuracy of the information contained therein
- Signature line and date

For instance, Alabama's format for filing the Articles of Incorporation can be accessed through the state's Secretary of State Corporate Division website (**www. sos.alabama.gov/downloads/business/sosdf-1.pdf**). The website contains instructions for filling out and submitting the document along with corresponding filing fees.

**STATE OF ALABAMA**
**DOMESTIC FOR-PROFIT CORPORATION**
**ARTICLES OF INCORPORATION GUIDELINES**

INSTRUCTIONS:

STEP 1: CONTACT THE OFFICE OF THE SECRETARY OF STATE AT 334-242-5324 TO RESERVE A CORPORATE NAME.

STEP 2: TO INCORPORATE, FILE THE ORIGINAL, TWO COPIES OF THE ARTICLES OF INCORPORATION, AND THE CERTIFICATE OF NAME RESERVATION IN THE COUNTY WHERE THE CORPORATION'S REGISTERED OFFICE IS LOCATED. THE SECRETARY OF STATE'S FILING FEE IS $40. PLEASE CONTACT THE JUDGE OF PROBATE TO VERIFY FILING FEES.

PURSUANT TO THE PROVISIONS OF THE ALABAMA BUSINESS CORPORATION ACT, THE UNDERSIGNED HEREBY ADOPTS THE FOLLOWING ARTICLES OF INCORPORATION.

*Article I*      The name of the corporation: _____

*Article II*     The duration of the corporation is "perpetual" unless otherwise stated.

*Article III*    The corporation has been organized for the following purpose(s): _____
_____

*Article IV*    The number of shares, which the corporation shall have the authority to issue, is _____.

*Article V*     The street address (NO P.O. BOX) of the registered office: _____
_____,
and the name of the registered agent at that office: _____.

*Article VI*    The name(s) and address(es) of the Director(s): _____
_____

*Article VII*   The name(s) and address(es) of the Incorporator(s): _____
_____

Any provision that is not inconsistent with the law for the regulation of the internal affairs of the corporation or for the restriction of the transfer of shares may be added.

IN WITNESS THEREOF, the undersigned incorporator executed these Articles of Incorporation on this the _____ day of _____, 20_____.

Printed Name and Business Address of Person Preparing this Document:

Type or Print Name of Incorporator _____

Signature of Incorporator _____

Rev. 7/03

Sometimes, finding the correct office within the state government's structure that best applies to your needs can be a challenge. The same office may have a different name in different states. In this case, the name of the office that provides services to businesses and corporations may be called Division of Corporations in one state, Business Services in another, Business Formation and Registration in another, and so forth. Therefore, to save you time and frustration while trying to establish a business, here is a shortcut so you can reach the appropriate office for filing Articles of Incorporation without having to search though the maze of governmental agencies in your state:

| State | Secretary of State's Office (specific division within) |
|-------|--------------------------------------------------------|
| Alabama | Corporations Division |
| Alaska | Corporations, Businesses, and Professional Licensing |
| Arizona | Corporation Commission |
| Arkansas | Business / Commercial Services |
| California | Business Portal |
| Colorado | Business Center |
| Connecticut | Commercial Recording Division |
| Delaware | Division of Corporations |
| Florida | Division of Corporations |
| Georgia | Corporations Division |
| Hawaii | Business Registration Division |
| Idaho | Business Entities Division |
| Illinois | Business Services Department |
| Indiana | Corporations Division |
| Iowa | Business Services Division |
| Kansas | Business Entities |
| Kentucky | Corporations |
| Louisiana | Corporations Section |
| Maine | Division of Corporations |

| State | Secretary of State's Office (specific division within) |
|-------|--------------------------------------------------------|
| Maryland | Secretary of State |
| Massachusetts | Corporations Division |
| Michigan | Business Portal |
| Minnesota | Business Services |
| Mississippi | Business Services |
| Missouri | Business Portal |
| Montana | Business Services |
| Nebraska | Business Services |
| Nevada | Commercial Recordings Division |
| New Hampshire | Corporation Division |
| New Jersey | Business Formation and Registration |
| New Mexico | Corporations Bureau |
| New York | Division of Corporations |
| North Carolina | Corporate Filings |
| North Dakota | Business Registrations |
| Ohio | Business Services |
| Oklahoma | Business Filing Department |
| Oregon | Corporation Division |
| Pennsylvania | Corporation Bureau |
| Rhode Island | Corporations Division |
| South Carolina | Business Filings |
| South Dakota | Corporations |
| Tennessee | Division of Business Services |
| Texas | Corporations Section |
| Utah | Division of Corporations and Commercial Code |
| Vermont | Corporations |
| Virginia | Business Information Center |
| West Virginia | Business Organizations |

| State | Secretary of State's Office (specific division within) |
|---|---|
| Washington | Corporations |
| Washington, D.C. | Corporations Division |
| Wisconsin | Corporations |
| Wyoming | Corporations Division |

# S Corporation

An S corporation is a form of legal structure; under IRS regulations designed for the small businesses, S corporation means small business corporation. Until the inception of the limited liability company form of business structure, forming S corporations was the only choice available to small business owners that offered some form of limited liability protection from creditors, yet afforded them with the many benefits that a partnership provides. Operating under S corporation status results in the company being taxed close to how a partnership or sole proprietor would be taxed, rather than being taxed like a corporation.

Operating under the S corporation legal structure, the shareholders' taxes are directly impacted by the business's profit or loss. Any profits or losses the company may experience in any one year are passed through to the shareholders, who in turn must report them as part of their own income tax returns. According to the IRS, shareholders must pay taxes on the profits the business realized for that year in proportion to the stock they own.

In order to organize as an S corporation and qualify as such under IRS regulations, the following requirements must be met:

- ▶ It cannot have more than 100 shareholders.
- ▶ Shareholders are required to be U.S. citizens or residents.
- ▶ All shareholders must approve operating under the S corporation legal structure.

▸ The company must be able to meet the requirements for an S corporation the entire year.

Form 253, "Election of Small Business Corporation," must be filed with the IRS within the first 75 days of the corporation's fiscal year.

Electing to operate under S corporation status is not effective for every business. However, it has proved to be beneficial for a number of companies through many years of operation. Because of the significant role S corporations play in the U.S. economy, The S Corporation Association of America was established in 1996 serving as a lobbying force in Washington, protecting the small and family-owned businesses from too much taxation and government mandates. Membership in the association is composed of S Corporations, both big and small, from throughout the nation. This includes companies such as the Barker Company, a family-owned business that makes custom cases used for refrigerated and hot displays found at supermarkets and convenience stores based in Keosauqua, Iowa. Another example is the Sumner Group, headquartered in St. Louis, Missouri. The Sumner Group is one of the largest independently owned office equipment dealerships in the nation.

# Bonding & Business Insurance

Being bonded and insured is a basic requirement for all notaries. Being bonded means a company has money available to cover claims filed by a customer. Insurance protects the business from injury claims by people on your business property or while conducting notary business on behalf of your company. This is an area you must be well versed in — especially if you work as an independent contractor.

Notaries should also obtain errors and omissions insurance to cover notary errors. This type of insurance protects notaries from claims made by customers that you made in error while performing your notary duties or claims that you failed to perform the work you were contracted to perform.

The coverage with an errors and omissions insurance policy typically covers legal expenses and judgments. Errors and omissions insurance covers you as an owner, as well as any employees or subcontractors you use for your notary business.

# Small Business Startup Checklist

Below are some steps you should take before opening the doors of your new notary business. Carefully consider each of the steps below and make sure you address all the aspects of opening your business honestly. You need to decide what will work best for you and your new business.

## *Identify the scope of your business and your goals.*

What products and/or services will you offer your clients? What are your short-term and long-term goals for your business? Do you have the necessary skills and knowledge in the area of specialty of your business? Do you have experience in the operation of a small business? Consider taking some business courses, reading some books, and even bringing in a partner who has the business know-how to help you succeed. Some helpful websites to reference include the U.S. Small Business Administration site, **www.sba.gov**, as well as a guide for *10 Steps to Starting a Business*, **http://www.business.gov/start/start-a-business.html**.

# Choosing a Business Name

Now that you have chosen what kind of business you want to form, the next step is to select a name. Your business name should reflect the kind of services you offer (notary-related) and can incorporate your name or your location. The name you choose should be something that you are happy operating as for years to come. Here are some examples to get you thinking about names for your business:

Sole proprietorship notary-based business names:

- ▶ Jane Doe Notary Services
- ▶ Doe Notary Services

Partnership notary-based business names:

- ▶ Doe and Smith Notary Services
- ▶ Doe and Smith Signing Agent Services

Location-based notary names:

- ▶ Florida Notary Services
- ▶ Florida Signing Agent Services
- ▶ Miami's Best Notary Services

Miscellaneous notary business names:

- ▶ Reliable Notaries
- ▶ The Nomadic Notary
- ▶ Acme Notary Service

Be aware of the following when choosing your business name:

- ▶ Does the name already exist? If so, it is best to choose a different name. You do not want to be confused with an already existing business, and you do not want any legal problems with an existing company for stealing or using its name. You can go to state corporation bureaus and secretary of state offices to see if a name is in use, or try checking the United States Patent and Trademark Office's free trademark database, **www.uspto.gov/trademarks/index.jsp**.

- ▶ Does the name clearly define the scope of your services? If not, your potential clients may not consider you when they need notary services because your name does not reflect the services you provide. Because you are offering notary services, it is a good idea to make sure the word "notary" is somewhere in your business name.

▶ Is your business name easy to say and spell? If not, your customers might not know how to locate you online, in the phone book, or on a map. Keeping things simple is often the best way to go when it comes to naming your business.

▶ Do not be overly creative when it comes to naming your business. You want your clients to take you seriously and view you as a professional at all times. Keep the wordplay at a minimum. Having a name that is too creative can also confuse people, because they will not be able to determine what kind of business you are operating if your business name is "Cutie Cathy's."

## Fictitious name registration

If your business name is different than your real name, most states require that you file a fictitious name registration, doing business as (DBA) registration, or some form of similar registration that specifies that the name you are using to conduct business is not your own. The agency with which the fictitious name or DBA name is filed varies from state to state. In some states, the registration is done with the city or county in which the company has its principal place of business. However, the majority require the registration to be done with the state's secretary of state's office. The only states that specifically do not require any type of filing when conducting business with a name other than your personal name are Alabama, Arizona, Kansas, Mississippi, New Mexico, and South Carolina. Washington, D.C., makes it optional, and Tennessee does not require such filing for sole proprietorships or general partnerships.

# Logos & Trademarks

Once you have determined your company name, you are ready to create an image for your business. Creating an image is about how you want your company to be perceived by the general public, customers, and suppliers. A business image is how people identify with and relate to the essence of your company. Part of creating and developing your image is cultivating your company's professional attitude, culture, and business ethics.

An integral part of this image is your business logo. The logo must be unique and different from anyone else's, because the last thing you want is to have your company mistaken for another. Graphic artists, marketing agencies, and print shops are excellent places to go to for the design of your logo; make sure to ask them for a high-resolution digital copy so you can reproduce it for all your business stationery and marketing needs. In addition to being able to find an abundance of graphic artists on the Internet, marketing agencies and print shops have graphic artists on staff or resources you can turn to. You also will be able to find marketing agencies and printing companies on the Internet or in your local community.

A trademark for a notary business is a word, symbol, phrase, or sound that represents the company and service to the public. Many trademarked logos and symbols are widely recognized, such as the McDonald's golden arches, the Pepsi logo, and the MasterCard logo. Examples of trademarked sounds are the chimes for the broadcast network NBC™ and the Yahoo!® yodel. Your brand name, logo, or other symbol(s) differentiate your company from a competitor. To be protected, the mark must either be used in commerce or registered with the intent to use it. Though use in commerce is sufficient to establish trademark rights, registration with the United States Patent and Trademark Office (USPTO) can strengthen trademark enforcement efforts. The letters TM in superscript (™) next to a word, brand, or logo used in commerce is sufficient to designate that the word, brand, or logo is trademarked. The TM is the designation for a unregistered trademark. A trademark that has been registered with the USPTO is designated with the R with a circle around it (®), also presented in superscript after the word or symbol. Use of the registered symbol for a nonregistered trademark could interfere with the right of an inventor to subsequently register the mark.

Trademark searches can be done professionally for between $300 and $1,200. Nevertheless, you can avoid these charges by using the Internet. Search registered and pending trademarks at the USPTO website (**www.uspto.gov**) and use the

Trademark Electronic Search System (TESS). Go to the New User Form Search, type in the name you want to use, and click "Search Term." Be certain that the "Field" term is on "Combined Word Mark." To make sure that your search is comprehensive, be certain to perform the following:

- Enter all phonetically similar names of your company, because phonetically similar names can cause conflicts in trademark use. For example, if you want to name your company "Netflicks," you should enter "Netflix" as well.

- Enter the singular and the plural of your company's proposed name.

- If your proposed name has more than one word, enter each word separately.

- Use "wild card" search terms, such as the asterisk (*) to broaden your search. For example, if you are searching for "Netflicks," you can enter "Netfli*" to search for similar names that began with the same six letters.

Be advised that trademark searches are not foolproof. Searches reveal only those names that are registered. Unregistered business names may be in use as well. It is considered valid even if the trademark or registered information does not show up in the USPTO database. Consequently, after searching there, you should search the Internet for the proposed name. This would probably reveal any current users of your proposed name. If you have reached this stage without discovering any conflicting trademarks or service marks, you should then search the secretary of state's records for existing corporate names. Most states offer free searches of existing corporate names.

If your name passes the previous tests, you may want to reserve it. This step is not necessary, but is recommended as you move through the planning and development stages of your new business. Most states offer a reservation service where you file a short name reservation form with the secretary of state, but the fee for this service will vary with each state. When you have finalized your name, make sure that you have an appropriate corporate suffix to make the public aware of your limited liability protection if you have decided to incorporate your business. Include:

▶ Corporation or Corp.

▶ Incorporated or Inc.

▶ Limited or Ltd.; in some states this suffix can be confused with a "limited partnership" or "limited liability company."

## Intent to use trademark registration

You can register a trademark with the USPTO prior to use in commerce, thereby establishing priority for the mark, if the inventor plans to use the trademark in commerce relatively soon. Initial registration is good for six months and can be extended (for a fee) for up to three years. If the trademark is not used before the intent-to-use registration expires, the trademark is considered abandoned. It then becomes available for others to use.

In most circumstances, trademarks and logos contain value. Think about the Olympic rings. The rings appear on a variety of products licensed by the International Olympic Committee. Consumers relate top athleticism and sportsmanship to these rings. Shoe manufacturers and other types of companies pay big bucks to associate with the Olympic mark to capitalize on the goodwill that the mark brings up in consumers' minds. Brand identity is an enormous marketing tool, one that should be built up and protected.

## Registering your mark

Though your mark acquires legal protection as soon as it is used in commerce, and the strength of that protection is based on its distinctiveness, there is still some additional protection to be had by registering your mark. About ¼ of all marks used in business are registered. If you develop a catchy brand name for your business or service, you may wish to register the name with an intent-to-use trademark application that will protect your right to use the mark.

The benefits of registration include:

▶ Providing patent attorneys and judges with more tools for enforcing protection of your mark

▶ Making it easy for others who want to use a similar or identical mark to find that it is in use

▶ Having the ability to prohibit infringing Internet domain names

▶ Giving judges the ability to levy additional monetary damages for mark infringement

▶ Enabling judges to restrain on infringing parties, preventing them from using the mark while you await a ruling on your rights

Just like claims in a patent, your mark may have several elements, including a combination of words, punctuation, color, and images. Each element should be examined independently to determine which is the strongest. Just as someone could engineer around your patent by omitting a single claim, someone might copy part but not all of your mark. If you select the strongest element of your mark — the component likely to have the broadest legal protection and register it — anyone who uses that component will be infringing.

If a word itself rather than the style it is written in is the mark, it is called typed format. The way the word is written, either the script or the combination of upper and lower case letters, is called a stylized or design format. A logo is known as a graphic mark.

Trademark law can be as arcane and convoluted as patent law, and retaining an intellectual property attorney to review your application, if not write it for you, is advisable. Once you file an application to register your mark, the process of having that mark approved will take about 18 months. Several rounds of objections and responses may take place in trademark registration just as they are likely to do in a patent application. This is an important state in which to have legal advice.

Reasons why a mark may be refused registration by the USPTO's examiners include possibility of confusion with an existing mark and lack of distinctiveness; it could be just too generic. In this case, you can request your mark be placed on what is known as the Supplemental Register. This list protects your priority for the mark while you use it in trade and hope that it acquires distinctiveness through association with your product in consumers' minds over time. Placing a mark on the Supplemental Register is tantamount to admitting your mark is not protectable. You may retain a chronological priority with the USPTO, but you will not be able to make a good case in court that your mark has been infringed.

When your mark is first approved, it is granted preliminary approval and enters a period in which others can challenge or object to your mark's registration. If someone believes your mark is infringing on their mark or is offended by your mark, they may file an objection. This will trigger an appeal before a trademark board. To pursue registration, you will have to hire an attorney to argue your case. If your mark is refused registration, you can appeal the examiner's decision with the assistance of an attorney.

Once your trademark is registered, you must use the registered trademark symbol. Without the notice of trademark, you still have legal protection to stop infringement on your mark, but judges may not be able to impose damages on the infringer.

Though trademark protection lasts for as long as the mark is in use, USPTO registration lasts six years. To extend the registration period, apply for an extension by providing evidence and a sworn statement that your mark is still in use. After the first renewal, your mark will remain registered for ten years and must be renewed at that interval.

## Register your business

Whether you decide to form a sole proprietorship or partnership, you will need to register your business with your secretary of state's office. The form of business you choose determines the amount of regulatory documents you have to file, and more important, the amount of taxes you have to pay. If you are caught running a business that has not been registered, you will be fined.

# Obtain an Employer Identification Number (EIN)

All employers, partnerships, and corporations must have an employer identification number (EIN), also known as a federal tax identification number. You must obtain your EIN from the IRS before you conduct any business transactions or hire any employees. The IRS uses the EIN to identify the tax accounts of employers, certain sole proprietorships, corporations, and partnerships. The EIN is used on all tax forms and other licenses. To obtain one, fill out Form 55-4, available from the IRS at **www.irs.gov/businesses/small**. Click "Small Business Forms and Publications." There is no charge. If you are in a hurry to get your number, you can get an EIN assigned to you by telephone, at 800-829-4933.

Also request the following publications, or you can download them via the Internet at **www.irs.gov**:

1. Publication #15, circular "Employer's Tax Guide."

2. Several copies of Form W-4, "Employer Withholding Allowance Certificate." Each new employee must fill out this form.

3. Publication 334, "Tax Guide for Small Businesses."

4. Request free copies of "All about OSHA" and "OSHA Handbook for Small Businesses." Depending on the number of employees you have, you will be subject to certain regulations from this agency. Their address is: O.S.H.A., U.S. Department of Labor, Washington, D.C. 20210, **http://osha.gov**.

5. Request a free copy of "Handy Reference Guide to the Fair Labor Act." Contact: Department of Labor, Washington, D.C. 20210, **www.dol.gov**.

The IRS website, Small Business Resource Guide, has been specifically designed to better assist the small business owner and those who are just starting up their new business venture. This guide can be accessed online at

**www.hud.gov/offices/osdbu/resource/guide.cfm.** Through this website, new business owners can access and download the necessary forms and publications required by the IRS.

## Seek legal and/or financial advice.

If necessary, consult a lawyer and/or accountant to write up a business agreement if you are forming a partnership. This will alleviate headaches and problems that may arise later.

## Establish funds.

You need startup cash to purchase supplies, advertise your services, and hire employees. Sources for funding can be found through governmental grants, private grants, or small business loans from a bank.

Venture capitalists, who can also provide aid with funding, are professional investors. They invest heavily in businesses in the hopes of earning a large return on their investment in the shortest time possible. You can expect their relationship with your business to be very "hands on," so be prepared for this if you look to a venture capitalist for financial support.

Another source of financial aid is the angel investor. Angel investors are individuals who are high-net-worth investors. They invest in business by looking for the highest return possible to compensate them for their risk. They generally have strong connections to several industries and know all the ins and outs of business negotiation, including various laws and contract negotiation. You need to think big when you sketch out your business idea; this is especially true when you make a proposal to an angel investor. They are looking for large returns over the shortest possible time, which often means more initial investment and an aggressive and progressive business plan.

Because starting a notary business has nominal costs involved, most notaries start a business using their own cash savings.

# Find a suitable location for your business.

You have two choices when deciding to open a new business: Do you want to work from home, or do you want to find office space? Working from home is a good option when you are just starting your business because the startup costs are lower, and it is more convenient. This is especially true if you intend on going to the client to notarize documents. However, once you expand your business and have a steady stream of clients, you may find it more convenient to have the customers come to you, and a home office may not be a safe or professional option.

When deciding where to locate your office, do your research to ensure the location you choose is a high-traffic area and also an area that does not already have several of the same types of businesses that you are planning on opening.

You can use the following list to evaluate a potential business site:

- Downtown area
- Historical district
- Business district
- Government offices
- Colleges/universities
- Technical schools
- Religious schools
- Military bases
- Hospitals
- Major highway
- Hotels
- Shopping

Evaluate these specifics about any location you are considering:

- How many similar notaries are located in the area?
- Find sales volume (check business licenses for previous year).
- Are there colleges or student housing in the area?
- Are there a high number of working mothers in the area?
- What is the population of the immediate area?
- Is the population increasing, stationary, or declining?
- Are there residents of all ages — old, middle-aged, or young?
- What is the average sales price and rental rates for area homes?
- What is the per capita income?
- Find the average family size.
- Is the building/location suitable for a notary establishment?

Once you find office space, you will have to decide whether to rent or lease this space. More about home offices and finding office space will be discussed in the next chapter.

C H A P T E R   7 :

# Establishing an Office

*N*ow it is time to choose where you will establish your notary office. Decide whether you want to run the business from your home or if you need to rent office space. As is the case with almost every decision you make in the business, there are pros and cons to establishing a home-based office and in setting up an office outside the home.

Notaries typically perform their work at the client's location, so most notaries starting out in business choose the cost effectiveness and convenience of running the notary business out of their home rather than renting an office space. Three other choices generally exist for establishing a notary business space: rent an office space, use a flextime office rental space, or share a space.

## The Home Office

Opening as a home-based business may be the most logical choice when it comes to financing your endeavor. After all, if you are already paying rent or a mortgage then it does not cost you any additional money to set up your home office. Two key elements to keep in mind when deciding if a home office is the right set up for you are determining whether you have the space and privacy in your home to conduct business.

So, take on the space issue first. If you live alone in a one- or two-bedroom apartment, then you can set up your business in the corner of your dining room or in the guest bedroom. If you live with other people, then you need to be able to shut out the rest of the world when it is time to talk to a client on the phone or concentrate on your work. Generally, to run a notary business, you only need an office that is large enough to hold your desk, chair, computer, printer, and phone.

Being a notary is either a part-time or full-time way of earning income, so it is important to treat your career seriously. If your home office is the home dining room table that you have to clear every night so your family can eat dinner, then the situation is probably not conducive to running your business and serving as your office. Spare bedrooms, a den, garage, the attic, or a finished basement are all viable options for a home office, which provides the dedicated space you need to work. You can leave your work one night and come back to it the next day and pick up right where you left off.

Kids, spouses, and pets may all be wonderful to have in your life, but can also equate to major distractions and interruptions when you are trying to work from home. When you are evaluating whether a home office is right for your business, consider privacy. Does the space you are considering transforming into your office allow you to work, make phone calls, and talk with clients without the interruption of your domestic life creeping in? There are also some financial benefits to consider when establishing a home office.

The IRS allows you to write off a space in your home that serves as an office full time. Generally, if your home office takes up ten percent of the total square footage of your home, then you are able to write off ten percent of your mortgage (principal and interest) or rent amount, which can offer a significant tax deduction. In order to write off the amount of your rent or mortgage though, the entire room has to be dedicated to your business.

## The Pros

▸ Saves you from having to pay rent for an office.

▸ Convenient and saves time and money because you do not have to commute.

▸ Provides a federal tax deduction when you have dedicated space for your office in your home.

## The Cons

▸ Blurs the line between your personal and business life.

▸ Is not conducive for times when you have to meet with clients.

▸ Requires installation of additional phone lines and uses space in the home for business purposes.

## Home Office Checklist

❏ Do you have an enclosed or private area (preferably with a door) where you can shut out the outside world when it is time to work?

❏ Does the home office provide enough space for a desk, computer, printer, and phone?

❏ Do you have the ability to add another phone line to the office?

❏ Is the space heated and air-conditioned?

❏ Do you have storage space for file and supplies?

# Flextime Office Space

In most medium and large cities, there are flextime office spaces or shared rental spaces as an option for setting up your notary business, which can typically be found in the Yellow Pages of your local phone book. Some flextime offices have "flex" in the name, but others use the term "executive" in the listing name. Shared space options allow you to rent a cubicle or office for a monthly fee. In addition to having your own dedicated workspace, these facilities also offer a receptionist to answer your business calls and forward the calls to you wherever you are or to take a message if you are unavailable. Generally, shared space options also provide limited administrative support to help you with tasks such as making copies, sending faxes, and creating correspondence. The flex space also provides you with a business mailing address where clients can send mail and packages and someone at the location to sign for and accept these deliveries.

A flextime office space provides your business with a professional façade. Rather than answering your own phone, a receptionist answers it for you. When clients need to come to you, you have a professional setting to conduct business. It also provides a place to go to everyday to complete your work, which some people need in order to get motivated and take care of business. Some flextime offices also allow renters to obtain space on an as-needed basis. Rather than pay a monthly fee for a dedicated space, you may have the option to use the facilities when and if you need them. You may opt for the mail and receptionist services to give off a professional appearance to clients and prospective clients calling your office and then book office space or a conference room when you need it.

## The Pros

▸ Provides a professional front

▸ Includes office furniture and supplies

▸ Some administrative support.

▸ Offers a dedicated workspace in a professional environment

▸ Reduces the cost of having to rent an entire office on your own

▸ Reduces the cost of having to hire staff, such as a receptionist or administrative support

## The Cons

▸ Costs can range from a couple hundred to $1,000 a month.

▸ There may be limitations on the personal items you can leave behind because other tenants share the space.

▸ The space has office hours, so if you need to work in off hours, you probably are not going to be able to access the building.

## Flextime Office Space Checklist

❏ What space is available to you?

❏ What office equipment is included?

❏ Do you have to pay a monthly fee, or can you rent on an as-needed basis?

❏ Is there a dedicated line for your business? If yes, does your fee payment include someone to answer the line, take messages, and transfer the calls to you?

❏ Do you have storage space for files and supplies?

# Shared Office Space

Along similar lines as flex office space, you may also consider sharing office space with another professional, such as an accountant, attorney, title company, or real estate office. Many professional service firms rent and occupy office space that is too large for its immediate needs, leaving empty office space unused. At times, these types of professionals are willing to rent out the extra space, which can mean that you obtain an office inside one of these offices or buildings at a reduced rate. Depending on your negotiations with the professional you are renting the space from, you may even be able to share a receptionist and administrative support services.

## The Pros

▸ Provides a professional environment at a lower rate than renting your own office

▸ Allows you to separate your business and personal life

▸ Depending on the type of firm you rent from, it may be a referral source of business for you.

## The Cons

▸ You have to commute to work.

▸ Shared items, such as the fax machine and the sign on the office, have the name of the firm you are renting from rather than your business name.

▸ Creates a rental payment that you would not have with a home office

## Shared Office Space Checklist

❏ What space is available to you?

❏ What office equipment is included (desk, computer, printer, and phone)?

❏ What is the monthly payment?

❏ Is there a dedicated phone number for your business? If yes, does your rent include someone to answer the line, take messages, and transfer the calls to you?

❏ Can you place a business sign outside the office door or on the building?

# Formal and Professional Office

The final option for setting up your business is to rent, lease, or buy an office space in an existing building or as a stand-alone building. Options for obtaining a formal office space can range from renting an office condo, floor, or office space in an office building to obtaining a retail space occupied by other stores and professionals, such as real estate and insurance agents. This gives you the option to couple your businesses and gain more exposure. Because these types of businesses have a need for notarized documents, you have the same audience and a better chance of landing business when clients need items notarized. The majority of these options come completely unfurnished and without any type of support staff, so you will have to furnish the office and hire staff as needed. The primary disadvantage to having a formal office is the cost involved in establishing and maintaining the office.

## Costs

Some of the costs you need to consider before deciding on a formal office space include:

▸ Upfront costs and down payment for a mortgage, lease, or rental payment (a percentage of the purchase price or first, last, and current month's rent payment)

▸ Insurance costs for keeping the office (liability, fire, theft)

▸ Installation of phone lines

▸ Purchase of furniture, equipment, and office decorations

▸ Alarm system and locks

▸ Employment of administrative staff

▸ Housekeeping/cleaning services

▸ Amenities such as a refrigerator, coffee maker, and microwave

## The Pros

▸ Provides a professional work environment

▸ Gives your business further exposure

## The Cons

▸ Distractions, such as package deliveries, the cleaning crew, and your administrative staff

▸ More expensive than any other office option available

## Formal Office Space Checklist

❏ What else does the rental space include (water, utilities)?

❏ What is the monthly payment?

❏ On top of the rental payment, what is it going to cost for electricity, phone service, cleaning, staffing, and other expenses?

❏ Will I need to hire staff to help run the office? If yes, how much will this cost for salary and benefits?

❏ Can you place a business sign outside the office door or on the building?

❏ Is the office a short commute from my home?

❏ Is the office conveniently located for business meetings with clients and vendors?

❏ Is the office located near related businesses that may be a referral source for business?

# Furniture, Equipment, and other Business Essentials

Whether you decide to establish your notary business in a home office or rent an office space, you need to determine what furniture, business equipment, and other supplies you need to get your business up and running and operating on a daily basis. These are the minimal necessities you need to get started. As your business continues to grow, your needs may, and probably will, change. This applies to office-related items rather than the notary supplies discussed in Part I of this book.

## *Phone*

The primary business tool you need for your notary business is a telephone — a dedicated phone number for your business, especially if you are working from a home office. The last thing you want is a client calling in the middle of dinner or in the middle of the night and disrupting your personal family time. You may wish to have a telephone with at least two lines or one line with call-waiting service. It is unprofessional for a client to call your office and receive a busy signal, so you want to make sure that even if you are on the phone, your clients can still get through to you or to voice mail. Along the same lines, you also want to have voice-mail service connected to your business phone. Voice mail helps you capture client messages when you are on the other line or do not answer.

A notary is often out of the office traveling to and from client locations, so you also need to have a reliable cell phone or smart phone to conduct business. You may or may not choose to hand out your cell phone number to clients, but a cell phone comes in handy for checking your office voice mail and handling business when and if you are on the road.

## Fax

You need to have fax capabilities, and there are a couple of different ways you can get the fax services you need. First, you can go the traditional route of buying a fax machine and installing a dedicated line in your office for the fax machine. This, of course, requires the purchase and maintenance the fax machine. An alternative route is to invest in an e-fax service where you can send and receive faxes online through your computer. There are several e-fax services that provide you with a dedicated phone number for your faxes, such as eFax® (**www.efax.com**), MyFax® (**www.myfax.com**), and RingCentral® (**www.ringcentral.com**). Instead of having to install a second phone line in your office, the e-fax service accepts the faxes for you and sends them to your e-mail. Opening your e-faxes is as easy as opening e-mail, and you can read the fax online or print it, if necessary. E-fax services also allow you to send faxes online. If you need to send a hard-copy document, you will need a scanner to scan the document into your computer. If you are faxing a word processing document or document already on your computer, then you can send it directly from your computer via fax. These services start at $20 a month with pricing depending on the monthly limitation of faxes you can send and receive.

## Printer, copier, fax, and scanner

All-in-one printer, copier, scanner, and fax machines may be a viable option for your office. Your other option is to buy separate machines for your printing, copying, faxing, and scanning needs. The good part of an all-in-one machine is that for a few hundred dollars or less you will have all the equipment you need. The downside is if one of the parts breaks then you either have to replace or repair the broken function of the machine or buy a replacement machine.

## Computer and computer software

You will need a computer for conducting Internet research, creating client correspondence, and more. If you have to buy a new computer, make sure that you invest in the best computer possible and that it has software capabilities such as word processing, spreadsheets, and database management.

You can purchase software such as Microsoft® Office, or you can investigate online (and free) options such as Google™ Docs (**http://docs.google.com**) where you can create and access documents online. Online offerings such as Google Docs also allow you to share and collaborate on documents with other parties. Even if your business turns you into a road warrior, other programs, such as Box (**www.box.net**), allow you to access your documents from any computer. As an added convenience, when you work on a document on one computer, it automatically backs up the update so you always have access to the most recent version of the document you are working on.

## Internet access

Internet access is an essential part of doing business. You will need Internet access for accessing your business e-mail, conducting research, and keeping up with what your competition is doing.

# Office furniture

Take inventory of some of the furniture you already own that you can use in your home-based or off-site office. At a very minimum, you need a desk and chair. You may also wish to have a bookshelf or storage area for client files and support materials. Most notaries find a need for a filing cabinet as well.

# Business supplies

The other basic business supplies you need may seem like obvious choices but are items that should not be overlooked as you set up your office.

- **Writing instruments:** Make sure you have a supply of your favorite pens and pencils on hand for everything from taking notes while on the phone with a client to signing client documents.

- **Paper:** First, standard copier paper and legal paper is a must for a notary office. You may wish to buy paper by the case or, at a minimum, by the ream. Second, you may want to have some fancier 24-pound paper on hand for creating letters to clients. Depending on your style, you may also want to have spiral-bound notebooks or pads of paper available.

- **Paper fasteners:** A stapler, staples, paper clips (large and small), binder clips, rubber bands, and tape are all notary office essentials. Preparing documents for clients in duplicate or stapling contracts together are but two of the reasons you need some fastening devices available.

- **Envelopes:** Generally, standard size No. 10 mailing envelopes are sufficient for mailing out everything from client invoices to contracts. You will find yourself mailing larger stacks of documents to lenders and such, so invest in 10- by 13-inch or 9- by 12-inch mailing envelopes as well. If you plan to run envelopes through your printer, make sure the envelopes are compatible with your printer.

▶ **File folders:** To maintain your files and records in a filing cabinet, you need hanging folders and file folders. Hanging and file folders come in various sizes and colors so you can try out different options to find the right ones for you or use a color coding system for your filing needs.

# Professional Help and Support

Once you have your office space chosen and stocked with the necessary equipment and supplies, it is time to build a network of professionals to help support and run your business. The extent of the support system you need to build depends on whether you are planning on being the sole employee of a home-based business or if you are establishing a formal off-site office. For example, if you plan on leasing an office space, you may need to hire someone to answer the phone and welcome walk-in traffic (deliveries, mail, maintenance, and cleaning), especially when you are out of the office during normal business hours. Even if you opt for a home-based business office, you will want to build a team of professionals to assist you.

The three primary support role positions you want to add to your team include a business banker, an accountant, and an attorney. Finding the best one available for your business can be a challenge, but it can also bridge the gap between your business and its success. These professionals usually have a broad range of experience working with various types of business owners. This can be beneficial to your company because they can provide advice to help you establish and run your business in the most beneficial manner possible. Having these types of professionals on your team can add a pool of referral business opportunities for your notary business because they work with documents in their own businesses that require notarization on a regular basis. When you begin your search for professionals, here are some things to keep in mind:

▶ **Experience and qualifications:** Try to avoid hiring someone who is a part-time lawyer, accountant, or banker. Focus on hiring professionals that are dedicated to the industry they serve. Make sure they have experience working with other notaries as well as with other types of business owners.

▶ **Availability:** It is important that the professionals you work with not have so many clients that they cannot fit you into their schedule.

▶ **Cost:** Cost is not the only factor, but it is a factor when deciding to work with a professional, so expect to pay more for professionals with more skill and experience than their competitors. Shop and compare professionals until you find the ones with the right experience and the right price for you and your business.

▶ **Integrity:** To build your notary business on high moral and ethical standards, you need to hire professionals who work with the same level of integrity.

▶ **Compatibility:** You also want to like the professionals you hire so you can work with them on a regular basis. Make sure you feel confident and comfortable working with the professionals you hire.

Because you may not hire someone with whom you have worked with before or know someone who has worked with them before, always ask for references and do your due diligence before hiring anyone. Try to obtain references that are similar to your business (home-based or notaries). Ask for and check at least three references from each professional you are considering. Checking references is not an option but a requirement to make sure that you are working with the right professional for your business. When checking references, be sure to ask questions such as what business the reference is in, how long they have been working with the professional, and how the professional has had a positive impact on their business.

# *Accountant*

There are some exceptions, but the majority of notaries starting and running a business are not accounting experts. Even if you are an accounting whiz, hiring an accountant is imperative to starting and maintaining the business financial records. Delegating this important duty to a professional allows you to focus on revenue generating business activities rather than worrying about paying your state sales tax, filing 1099 reports, or generating a profit and loss statement for your business.

One of the primary factors in small businesses failures is maintaining inaccurate and inefficient business and financial records. Having a professional accountant on your team can help ensure accurate records, and accurate records help keep your business on the path to success. The role of an accountant in a notary business typically consists of five main tasks:

1. **Small business startup accounting, sale of a business, or the purchase of a business:** An accountant can establish your business books and recordkeeping system so you start out on the right foot. When and if you sell your business, the accountant can help show the potential buyer and the buyer's accountant how financially sound the business is, where the profits for the business come from, and the assets and liabilities the business has. Finally, if you are purchasing an existing notary business, the accountant can review the financial records of the business to tell you if the purchase is a wise investment.

2. **Create and implement an accounting system:** A professional accountant can assess the needs of your business in order to create and implement an accounting system that best fits your business needs.

3. **Prepares, reviews, and audits the financial statements of the business:** Professional accountants have the know-how to accurately prepare your financial records to make sure you are compliant with the IRS and state

tax regulations. The accountant can also review and audit the company financial records to offer you advice on changes you need to make in your business and to ensure you are compliant with the laws in case you are ever audited.

4. **Tax planning and appeals:** Accountants are knowledgeable about many tax laws and loopholes, which they use to help you appropriately plan to minimize your tax obligations. If you run into a tax issue, the accountant also helps you prepare an appeal.

5. **Prepares income tax returns:** Businesses, depending on the legal structure of the business (sole proprietorship, corporation, LLC), have to file tax forms throughout the year, including annual federal business tax returns. The accountant prepares and files these forms on your behalf and makes sure you meet the deadlines for each tax form filing.

One of the best ways to find an accountant for your notary business is to ask family members and friends, especially those who have a small business, whom they use for their own tax needs. Interview accountants as you would any professional you are adding to your business support team, and make sure you shop around and compare several different accountants before deciding on which one is right for you.

You may be wondering what the difference is between an accountant and a certified public accountant (CPA). A CPA is a professional accountant that has taken and passed a state exam covering business law, accounting, taxes, and auditing. CPAs also are required to have a college degree, although some states allow CPAs to substitute work experience for a college degree.

Is a CPA better than an accountant for your notary business? It depends on your business needs. Professional accountants can be as sufficient as CPAs when it comes to establishing and maintaining your business books and financial records, so it is better to assess the experience of each accountant or CPA you interview and learn if his or her experience relates to your business needs.

## Lawyer

Even if your business is starting out with one employee (you), a lawyer is an essential member of your business support team. In fact, hiring an attorney is a task you may want to accomplish before you do anything else, including choosing the legal form of your business entity, because a lawyer can help guide you to establish your business in the most beneficial manner for your needs. The role of an attorney in your business can be as small or large as you choose it to be. Most people think of an attorney when they need court representation, but there are several additional roles attorneys can play, with some roles keeping you out of court in the first place. Attorney roles include:

- Helping you choose the right business structure
- Creating and reviewing business contracts
- Working on issues that may and do arise with employees
- Assisting with business credit issues, including bankruptcy
- Addressing client complaints and issues (major ones)

## Banker

With money playing a pivotal role in your notary business, it is no wonder that hiring a banking institution that fits your needs is imperative. Your business bank handles the checking and savings accounts for your business, but the role of the bank goes beyond these basic business needs. The bank also acts as the tax depository service for your business tax payments and may be a lender to your business if it needs funds to start, grow, or for another need. Generally, you want to establish a relationship with a bank that has a local presence so you have easy access to them when you need them. Financial institutions range from banks and credit unions to credit card, commercial finance, and consumer finance companies.

**Banking institutions:** Banks, savings and loans, and even commercial banks are traditional financial institutions that most businesses turn to when establishing various types of financial accounts. As a small notary company, you may wish to turn to the bank where you keep your personal accounts first to see what it offers in the area of business services. Because you already have an established relationship with the institution, it can make it easier and more convenient to handle your business transactions there as well.

**Credit unions:** Credit unions operate on a similar level to banks; the only difference is the members of the credit union own it. Credit unions tend to offer the same products and services as a traditional bank but at a reduced cost. The issue you may run up against with a credit union is that often times it offers personal accounts and services but may not offer the same extent of business products or services and, therefore, may not fit your business financial needs.

**Credit card companies:** In most cases, small business owners are personally responsible for credit card debt and loans for the business. Many notaries use business credit cards and business credit card loans to finance the startup costs of their business. The disadvantage to using this type of credit is that the interest rates are typically much higher than standard bank, credit union, and other business loans.

**Consumer finance companies:** Consumer finance companies lend to those who have bad credit, have defaulted on previous loans, or have a hard time obtaining a loan from more traditional lending institutions. These types of borrowers are higher risk for the finance company, so consumer finance companies tend to charge higher interest rates than other types of lending institutions, and the terms of the loan tend to be shorter and less attractive. Generally, a consumer finance company should be the last stop on your list and only if you cannot obtain credit or loans from one of the other types of institutions.

# Permits and Licenses

## City business license

You will almost certainly need a city business license if you are operating within a city, and you may need a county permit if not located within city boundaries. You can find out more about what licenses and permits you may need, where to get them, and how much they will cost by calling your city hall or county clerk's office. In most cities, the city clerk does not issue business licenses, but can direct you to the correct office if you cannot find it on your own.

You need a city license for several reasons, starting with the fact that you can be fined heavily for running a business without the correct permit. You also need to show your customers that you are legitimate, and you will need a city business license in most states to get your sales tax permit.

When you contact the agency that issues the city business license, ask how long the license is good for, what the renewal process is, whether there are levels of licensing, what level you need, how much it will cost, and whether there is anything else you need to do to operate as a legal notary business within your city or county.

## How to know you have covered it all

The best way to make sure you have everything done is to ask someone who knows you. SCORE and SBDC are good resources for this; you may also want to call your local chamber of commerce and ask whether someone can help you make sure you have covered everything for your startup licensing and permits. Talking with someone doing business in your area can be a big help in making sure that you are complying with all the relevant laws and regulations.

# CHAPTER 8:

# Create a Winning Business Plan

*B*usiness plans are your road map to success. The only way you can reach your goal of succeeding with your business is by having a plan. It is difficult at best to establish and operate a business when you do not quite know how to go about it — let alone trying to accomplish it without a thorough assessment of what you want to accomplish, how you plan to go about it, and what financial support you have to accomplish it. As you prepare to undertake the enormous task of starting a new business, evaluate your situation as it stands today and visualize where you want to be three to five years from now. To work your way from today's standpoint to owning and operating a successful business, you must set goals to reach along the way that will serve as benchmarks on your road to success.

The most important and basic information to include in a business plan include:

▶ State your business goals.

▶ Describe the approach you will take to accomplish those goals.

▶ Discuss what potential problems you may encounter along the way and how you plan to address those problems.

▶ Outline the organizational structure of the business (as it is today and how you plan it to be).

▶ State the capital or cash and goods you will use to generate income, to get started, and to keep your business in operation.

Various formats and models are available for developing business plans. There are even entire books devoted to guiding you through the development of a business plan. No two businesses are the same, and even though there may be some basic similarities, each business is as individual and unique as people. Therefore, even though it is recommended that you follow the basic structure of commonly used templates, you should customize your business plan to fit your needs. A number of websites provide a variety of samples and templates can be used as reference, such as **www.bplans.com**, **www.nebs.com/nebsEcat/business_tools/bptemplate**, and **www.planmagic.com**, to name a few.

When writing your business plan, focus on its ultimate purpose; consider the many reasons why the plan is developed and its possible applications. For instance, if you are not putting the plan together for a business loan, then a condensed version of the business plan can be created. The following business plan covers the basic structure of a generic business plan and incorporates key elements of the business.

# Parts of a Business Plan

## Cover page

The cover page should include the name of your company in all capital letters in the upper half of the page. Several line spaces down, write the title "Business Plan." Last, write your company's address, the contact person's name (your name), and the current date.

NAME OF COMPANY

Business Plan

Address

Contact Name

Date

# *Table of contents*

## *Body of the business plan*

## MISSION STATEMENT

It is very important that you present your business and what it is all about from the very beginning of your business plan. When writing your mission statement, three key elements that must be considered and discussed are: the purpose of your business, the goods or services that you provide, and a statement regarding your company's attitude toward your employees and customers. A well-written mission statement could be as short as one paragraph, but should not be longer than two.

## I. EXECUTIVE SUMMARY

The executive summary should be about one to two pages long and should be written last, because it is a summary of all the information included in the plan. It should address what your market is, the purpose of the business, where it will be located, and how it will be managed. Write the executive summary in such a way that it prompts the reader to look deeper into the business plan. It is a good idea to discuss the various elements of your business plan in the order you address them in the rest of the document.

## II. DESCRIPTION OF PROPOSED BUSINESS

Describe in detail the purpose of and what you intend to accomplish with the business plan. Describe your services and the role your business will play in the market. Explain what makes your business different from all the rest in the area and clearly identify the goals and objectives of your business. The average length for the proposed business description section is one to two pages.

# III. MANAGEMENT AND STAFFING

Clearly identifying the management team and any other staff that may be part of the everyday operations of the business will strengthen your business viability by demonstrating the business will be well managed. Keep in mind that employees are a company's greatest asset. State who the owners of the business are, as well as other key employees with backgrounds in the notary industry or other business experience. Identify the management team as well as any others you may need in the future to expand your business. For instance, it may be just you when starting; however, in your plans for expansion, you might think about incorporating someone well versed in marketing or putting together a team of notaries. The management and staffing section of the plan may be as short as one paragraph if you are the only employee or one to two pages depending on how many people you have and anticipate having as part of your staff.

# IV. MARKET ANALYSIS

The market analysis section should include research on the notaries already practicing in the area, the services being offered or the lack thereof, which means there is a need for notary services in the area that are currently going unfulfilled. With numerous sources of information available, both online and through printed media, you can acquire a wealth of knowledge about notary services in general as well as the need for these services in the geographic area you intend to cover. This process adds validity to your business because it prepares you to assess the needs you can fulfill, as well as answer any questions you may be asked by potential investors or lenders to fund your business. Essential elements include a thorough analysis of your direct competition in the area or possible needs that need to be filled; specific identification of your competition; and your intended strategy and approach to the market you are targeting. The market analysis element of your business plan should be one of the most comprehensive sections of the plan, which means it will most likely be several pages long, depending on the number of services, number of competitors, and the number of target markets. In particular, the Target Market section of this portion of the plan can easily be two to three pages.

## Industry Background

Provide a comprehensive description of the notary business as it relates to the segments of the market you are targeting. Include trends and statistics that reflect the direction the market is going and how you will fit into that movement. Discuss major changes that have taken place in the industry in the recent past, which will affect how you will conduct business. Provide a general overview of your projected customer base, such as businesses or types of consumers.

## Target Market

This is one of the largest sections of the business plan because you will be addressing key issues that will determine the volume of sales and, ultimately, the revenue that you will be able to generate for your business. Revenue encompasses the total amount of money received by a company for its goods or services. The target market is who your customer or groups of customers are. By this point, you have decided the role you will take on, so it is a good idea to narrow down your proposed customer base to a reasonable volume. If you try to spread your possibilities too thin, you may be wasting your time on efforts that will not pay off and end up missing real possibilities. Identify the characteristics of the principal market you intend to target, such as demographics, market trends, and geographic location of the market.

Discuss what resources you used to find the information on your target market. Elaborate on the size of your primary target market — your potential customers — by indicating the possible number of prospective customers, what their purchasing tendencies are in relation to your services, their geographic location, and the forecasted market growth for that particular market segment. Expand your discussion to include the avenues you will use to reach your market. Include whether you plan to use the Internet, printed media, trade shows, and/or other media. Explain the reasons why you feel confident that your company will be able to compete effectively in the industry. Discuss your pricing strategies and address potential trend changes in trends that may favorably or negatively impact your target market.

## Service Description

Do not describe the features of your service, but rather focus on describing how your service benefits or fills the needs of potential customers. Especially focus on your unique selling proposition (USP), which is the clear advantage your services have over your competition. For example, if the other notaries servicing the area have offices, but there is a need for a mobile notary service and that is how you intend to offer your services, then this is your USP.

## Market Approach Strategy

Describe how you plan to enter the market and carve out a niche. Determining how to enter the market and what strategy to use will be critical for breaking into the market.

## V. MARKETING STRATEGY

In order to operate a financially successful business, you must not only maintain a constant flow of income, but also boost your profits by increased sales. The best way to accomplish this is through an effective marketing program or plan, such as promoting your products and services by advertising, attending trade shows, and establishing a presence on the Internet, to name a few. The marketing strategy portion of the business plan identifies your current and prospective customers, as well as the means you will use to advertise your business directly to them. The marketing strategy portion of your business plan is likely to be several pages long — at least three to four pages — depending on how much detail you include in the plan. The marketing strategy includes the services you offer along with the pricing strategy for each service, sales plan, and the advertising and promotions plan for the services.

## Pricing Strategy

While the previous section of the plan listed your service menu, along with a description and benefits of the service, this area of the plan couples the pricing with each service. When pricing your services, you not only have to price the services in order to turn a profit, but also you have to consider how your competition is pricing their services. The most effective method of doing this is by gauging your costs, estimating the tangible benefits to your customers, and making a comparison of your services and prices to similar ones in the market.

You should also address why you feel the pricing of your services is competitive in comparison to others. If your price is slightly higher than that of the competition, then you need to justify why. In addition, you want to address the return on investment (ROI) you anticipate to generate with the pricing strategy and the time frame. ROI is a ratio calculation of how much of a monetary investment returns you in profit to the business.

# Your Services, Your Time, Your Income

Once you decide which services you want to incorporate in your business, you must decide how much to charge for your work. The rates you charge can vary depending on the state in which you perform notary duties and your qualifications and experience. Your revenue will be different than a person whose career is in administrative and support fields because you will not be working with billable hours; you will be paid per service you offer.

You cannot charge more than people are willing to pay. Research and see what other notaries are charging. Pay close attention to the number of notaries in your area. Within reason, you can approximate your income by formulating your billable hours per month times the rate you expect to charge.

# What Should You Charge?

Pricing formulas will change due to market conditions, as the laws of supply and demand come into play. How much do people want your services? It is not an easy thing to judge, which is why you should see what others are charging and be competitive. Competing with the prices of other companies combined with your business reliability, punctuality, and attention to detail will make your business profitable. Keep these things in mind when setting your price because customers often view good quality service as better than a good price.

Pricing in the notary business is fixed when it comes to certain areas of your service. Notaries, along with mobile notaries, typically make $10 per signature. You can charge extra for services for mileage — in case you are a mobile notary — or emergency or urgency fees. Mobile notary signing agents can make anywhere from $50,000 to $100,000 per year, according to the California Notary website, **http://gsn.notary.net/notary.cfm**.

Different jobs and services have different fees. For instance, when you do mortgage document signing (which is when someone has to sign loan documents that must be notarized), you get more than the usual fee. If you take those documents to somebody's home and notarize them, you are paid generously for it. Payments per signature range from $50 to $75, according to Notary.net, **www.notary.net/loansigningcompanies.cfm**. As with everything in business, being a mobile notary has its advantages and disadvantages; it all depends on how you view it, in terms of your business.

Should you decide to be a mobile notary, as an independent contractor you can set your own prices for mileage. If you are an employee, you do not have that luxury. Often, banks or mortgage companies reimburse you for less than you would have made as an independent mobile notary. How many signatures you have to notarize, where you have to travel for the business to take place, and if documents are urgent will determine how much you charge clients.

Mortgage signing usually generates the most income for an individual. The second most profitable would be loan document business signing and then the normal document signing. A notary could charge more for normal document signing depending on how far he or she needs to travel. This is why most notaries have additional jobs and notarize part time to supplement their income.

## How to establish the price-per-service fee

The average price per service means the amount charged per document and per signature. If two people are signing at the same time, there are two charges because the charge is to attest for a person, not a document. The notary has to check the person's ID and then put his or her identification information in his or her notary journal. The price varies by state, but the standard charge for one signature is $10. Many people complain about the charges, but they are not too high considering how much responsibility the notary has. The notary is liable if anything is missed or if there is a problem.

A notary public makes a substantial profit by notarizing and administering the signing of loan documents. The average pay for that is $250 per signing. With notaries being able to handle two to three of these transactions per day, a substantial sum of money can be made. The reason payment is so much more is because a person attesting to loan documents is taking more risk.

## Sales

Now that you have determined how to price your goods and services, it is time to think about how you are going to sell your services. Describe the system you will use for fulfilling client requests and billing your customers. Also, address what methods of payments you will take from customers, including credit terms and discounts, if applicable.

## Advertising and Promotion

Discuss how you plan to advertise your services and promote your business to a specific market. One of your goals in this section is to break down what percentage of your advertising budget is allocated to each aspect of online and offline marketing, such as through trade magazines, trade shows, and via a business website. Also, note the expected return on investment for each method.

# VI. OPERATIONS

Discuss the current and proposed location of the business, describing in detail any existing facilities. Discuss any equipment you currently have or require in order to start and expand the business. If you have employees, or anticipate having them, give a brief description of the tasks the employees will perform in providing the services to clients.

# VII. STRENGTHS AND WEAKNESSES

If there are numerous notary business owners in the market, all competing for the same prospects, those that survive are the ones that can put its strengths into place and work to overcome its weaknesses to gain position in the market. In this section of the plan, elaborate on the particulars of your business that have enabled you, and will continue to enable you, to be successful. Discuss those things that set you apart and give you an advantage over your competitors, such as your particular geographic location.

Every business has weaknesses and the weaknesses of your business have to be addressed in order to propel your business toward success. Some weaknesses may include inexperience and limited exposure to the market, both of which you can overcome. Each weakness should be discussed in detail and include a plan to overcome it. Although important, discussing strengths and weaknesses should not take away from other focal points of the business plan. Therefore, keep this section relatively short, no more than one page in length.

# VIII. FINANCIAL PROJECTIONS

Financial projections normally derive from pre-existing historical financial information. When you are preparing a business plan as part of your business startup process, historical financial data obviously will not be available, and working with estimates based on other notary business performance is typical. If you are using the business plan as part of the application process for a loan, then be sure to match your financial projections to the loan amount you are requesting.

When developing your financial projections, you must consider every possible expense, expected and unexpected, yet be conservative in your revenue estimates. An expense is any cost of doing business resulting from revenue-generating activities. It is not critical that your actual revenues exceed the estimated amount. However, it is not a good situation when expenses are more than expected. Your projections should be addressed for the next three to five years, breaking down each year with the following information: projected income statements, cash-flow statements, balance sheets, and capital expenditure budgets. An income statement shows a company's revenue, expenses, and income, or the difference between the two. A cash-flow statement depicts where a company's money is coming from and how it is being spent. A balance sheet provides a short explanation of a company's financial well-being; it contains the assets of a company (anything under ownership of the business worth money), liabilities (including creditor claims working against company assets), and net worth (total assets minus total liability). A capital expenditure budget outlines plans for funds to be used to acquire or improve physical assets, such as buildings, property, or equipment. Due to the nature of this section, you can anticipate it taking up several pages of your business plan.

## IX. CONCLUSION

The conclusion is the wrap-up of the entire plan. Use it to state your case wisely, highlighting key issues discussed in the plan. Close with a summary of your plans for the expansion and progress of your business. Use language that will help the reader visualize what you will be able to accomplish and how successful your business will be should you receive the support you are requesting.

## X. SUPPORTING DOCUMENTS

Attaching supporting documentation to your business plan strengthens it and makes it more valuable. However, do not overburden it with too many attachments; finding a balance is important. Before you start attaching documents, ask yourself if that particular piece of information will make a difference; if the answer is no, then leave it out. Documents that you should attach include:

- ▶ Copies of the resumes of the business principals
- ▶ Tax returns and personal financial statements of the principals for the last three years
- ▶ A copy of licenses, certifications, and other relevant legal documents
- ▶ A copy of the lease or purchase agreement, if you are leasing or buying office space

# CHAPTER 9:
# Managing Finances and the Business Budget

Once you get your business up and running, one of the pivotal pieces of running a successfully financial notary business is to be able to create and to stick to a budget and properly manage the finances.

## Cash Flow

Once you determine whom your clients are and what the fees are for your services, you can start to formulate an idea of where your income is going to come from, but the focus of this section is how the business income is used to pay the business bills. With a startup business, this is a projected cash-flow statement, so you can see how your expenses relate to your expected income. In order to create a cash flow statement, you need:

▶ **Fixed costs estimate:** This estimate looks at the fixed expenses on a month-by-month basis — for instance, rent, telephone, insurance, and fixed loan payments.

▶ **Variable costs estimate:** This estimate looks at the fluctuating costs of doing business, such as automobile fuel, office supplies, utilities, or equipment maintenance or repair, on a month-by-month basis.

▶ **Income projection:** This projection addresses how much you expect to generate in income.

▶ **Pricing structure worksheet:** This worksheet helps you calculate how much it costs per day for you to be in business.

Business success directly relates to sound money management: keeping careful track of the amount of money that comes in, where it comes from, how much money goes out, and where it goes. Ideally, you will calculate your best estimate of operating costs before you start your business and build in regular re-evaluations to ensure your estimates are on the mark once your business is underway.

You want to know your basic cost of doing business — the amount you need to remain solvent — *before* you add services. If the number is $5,000, and there are 30 days in a month, you must make an average of $167 each day of the month to pay your basic expenses. In other words, you are not making money or turning a profit until you exceed this amount.

Start by estimating what it costs you to be in business for one month. Add up fixed costs, such as rent, phones, and ongoing marketing expenses. Do not forget to add in the monthly travel expenses if you will be going to clients rather than having them come to you.

You will also need to figure employee wages, benefits, and many other costs. An accountant may be able to give you a more detailed approach to determine your costs. The point is to have a realistic method of determining costs so you will know how to factor them into your pricing.

# Taxes

Taxes are a critical factor in sound money management. It is essential to maintain records of all sales and expenses, down to the last penny. The IRS will want to see what came in and what went out, especially if your business undergoes an audit. Clear, up-to-date records show that you are a responsible taxpayer. Keeping accurate books is not only to answer to the government but also is a map of the financial life of your business. If you do not keep accurate and detailed numbers, you will not have any idea how your company is doing financially. You must have the numbers and understand them to know whether you are meeting your goals and are generating a decent profit.

Make sure to file your federal, state, and local taxes in a timely manner. In some places, you may be required to collect sales tax on your services. Verify these requirements by contacting your city or state tax department. They will tell you what licenses or tax filings are necessary, as well as the schedule and appropriate ways to file. Many taxing entities are converting to online tax filings for businesses. You will need to set up a special account on the related government website to use online filing and payment methods.

# Controlling Costs

Controlling costs is the most challenging aspect of business. You are in business to make money, but you must accomplish two things to do this: find customers who will pay you fairly for your services and control your business spending to enable you to make a profit. Many small business owners, especially new ones, find that their cash flow is out of control and, even though accounts receivable is healthy, they do not have the money on hand to pay bills or payroll on time. This is where budgeting and cost controls become critical.

Company cost controls begin with the first item you pay for, whether it is a license fee or a desk for your office. It is to your advantage to shop around, determine the going rate for your purchase, and look for discounts. A small accounting firm that specializes in small businesses may offer lower rates than a large firm that deals with large corporations.

Never blindly accept any price. Ask yourself how any product or service can be obtained for less money. As you put together your monthly, quarterly, and annual budgets and cost estimates, plan to spend as little as possible. When you start out in business, it is wise to stick to the basics. It may be tempting to be a bit extravagant here and there: a nice leather chair for your office or a fancier desk, but you cannot make money if you are spending it all.

# Breakdown of Costs

## Utilities

There are numerous ways to reduce your consumption of gas and electricity. It may seem inconsequential to save pennies on your electricity bill, but if you start there, the pennies will add up.

Low-energy light bulbs are good for the environment and use less electricity. If you have gas heat, make sure the system is working efficiently and has a clean filter. If you are working out of your home and are taking a tax deduction for your office space, be aware that basic cost efficiencies in your home will eventually translate into dollars for you. Enlist your utility company to perform an energy audit of your home and office, and heed the advice for cutting utility usage, therefore cutting expenses.

## Office expenses

If you can develop systems and strategies that keep your operating costs down, even a few cents at a time, it will add up in the long run. For example, professional-looking letterhead with a single color serves its purpose and is much less expensive than two- or full-color letterhead. Envelopes, business cards, order forms, contracts, and other forms can look crisp and professional without a high price tag. You can even print some forms yourself. You may buy office supplies online through a discount supplier or buy from an office supply warehouse. Buy in bulk if you will use a lot of the product, but avoid oversupply (especially if you have limited storage in your office).

If you lease equipment for services such as credit card processing and postage, shop around for the best deal. Practice your negotiating skills on every product and with all vendors. Keep in mind that every vendor you deal with has the same goals you have for your business: gaining the highest possible margins. Beware of unnecessary upgrades a company may try to sell, and keep your basic goal of quality in mind while covering the essentials.

## Controlling loan costs

If you borrow money to start the business or arrange for a line of credit to purchase equipment or smooth your cash flow, incorporate loan payments into the business budget. Seek the lowest interest rates and the best terms for the money and be aware that fees, closing costs, and document processing can raise the cost of borrowing money. If your credit is good, you will discover that most lenders are happy to deal with you and are willing to negotiate. If your credit is not so good, it may mean higher interest rates, increased fees, and special charges. Do your best to improve your credit score by borrowing as little as possible, paying on time and in full. If you maintain good financial habits, your credit score will rise, and the cost of borrowing money will go down.

## Controlling marketing costs

Marketing is essential to business, but it can be a budget buster. Your annual marketing plan is likely to include an ad in the Yellow Pages and similar publications. Avoid the temptation to go for a full-page advertisement, despite what a salesperson may tell you about its benefits. A Yellow Pages presence may be important, but you do not need to spend big dollars. There can be a significant lag time for such annual ads. If your business is like most startups, you will have a limited marketing budget. It is advisable to spread it around to get the best value and only choose marketing options that are worthwhile and truly have the chance to make the business money.

## Dues

Your membership in organizations such as the chamber of commerce, Business Networking International (BNI), and local or national professional groups will bring you business, so budget money to pay your dues. Plan to spend several hundred dollars per year for these memberships, plus whatever application or initiation fees are involved. Most of these groups will waive their fees at some period during the year as initiatives to increase membership.

If you find that the cost of membership in all of the groups you identify will not fit in your initial budget, determine which one or two of these organizations will be most beneficial, and delay joining the others. Talk to other professionals about the groups they have joined, and ask them which provide the most leads or customers. In some cases, BNI produces more residential business than the local chamber of commerce, but the chamber ultimately can offer business-to-business contacts that you might otherwise miss.

There is one unavoidable fact about memberships in business groups: You must show up and be active, or you will be wasting your money. Membership alone does not bring in business. You must go to the meetings, pass out your business cards, work a booth at the annual fund-raising picnic, volunteer for whatever charity your group supports, and help other members increase their businesses just as you are asking them to help you. This requires a commitment of time, which can be in short supply for a small business owner.

## Employees

If you choose to hire a full- or part-time employee, be aware that the cost can be far higher than you anticipate. You have two choices to get work done: Hire an employee for your company whose taxes are deducted by your company, or sign up someone who is an independent contractor for whom you would file a 1099 income tax form. A person working under a 1099 uses a federal tax ID or Social Security number, operates his own business, and is responsible for his own taxes.

This type of arrangement can save you money because it alleviates costs such as health insurance, Social Security taxes, and space to house the employee.

The IRS employer tax information is available in hard copy or online at **www.irs.gov/publications/p15/ar02.html**.

A full-time employee can be more expensive overall, and you have to follow labor department guidelines for overtime and other employee labor rules that are not relevant to contractors. One or more full-time employees on staff mean payroll considerations. It is a basic business assumption that employees make money for employers, so do the math to see if this is true for you. You must make enough to pay for employee salaries and a little more to pay for marketing, insurance, and all of the other costs of doing business before you break even. It is easier to add benefits than to take them away, so be cautious as you go through the hiring process. Your first responsibility is to your business.

## Cost of business

It takes money just to keep the doors open for business. There will be expenses to pay, whether you have customers or not. You have business cards to print, letterhead, utilities, and rent. These are the day-to-day expenses of operating a business. Major equipment purchases are one-time expenses, and the cost can be spread over time, but there is no getting around the need for tight budgeting of the everyday costs you will incur. Examine each category, and be tough in your budgeting. Look for ways to save money, and confine your spending to what your business needs, not what you want.

## Setting financial targets

While you are still planning to open your business, you should take the time to lay out an initial budget and do preliminary income forecasting with your banker and accountant. Set a particular target income for the first three years at a minimum. Then, work backward to figure out how many jobs you will need to reach that income level, and what you will do to find those customers. Taking a hard look at your income potential before you start places you in a realistic position from the beginning to build and maintain a profitable business.

## Evaluating your progress

Even though you have set targets and think you know where the money in your business will originate from, circumstances change. Re-evaluating your business on a monthly or quarterly basis, and then annually, helps assess how the business is doing and where changes may be necessary. You may want to enlist your accountant in this process to show you how to compare reports on your software accounting program and provide you with the information you need.

# Accounting 101

Accounting is one of the most important aspects of running a business. When you are planning your business and getting caught up with all of the wonderful dreams you have of being a business owner, accounting is probably not one of those dreams. Yet, without a rudimentary understanding of accounting, you will not survive.

Entrepreneurs who neglect the financial aspect of business realize when it is too late that the business is not making a profit. If you are unaware of your margins and cash flow, you can forget about succeeding in business.

## What is an accounting system?

An accounting system will move your business into the 21st century and provide you with important financial indicators. An accounting system includes the following parts:

**Data Collection:** Business transactions and operations data

**Data Organization:** The process of examining and sorting data by date and transaction type

**Accounting Database:** Inputting data into a spreadsheet or accounting software

**Financial Statements and Reports:** This includes all your basic business forms: balance sheets, income statements, budgets, and timetables.

**Analysis:** Periodic examination of your business to avoid problems and capitalize on opportunities

You will also need basic accounting forms to track your revenue. The following are basic forms to keep your finances in order:

▶ A balance sheet, which is a record of your assets, liabilities, and capital

▶ An income statement profit and loss (P&L), which summarizes your earnings, expenses, net profits, and losses

▶ Cash-flow projection statement, which provides you with the inflows and outflows of cash into your business

It is up to you to establish an accounting system. Once your accounting system is in place, there will be less stress, and you will rest easier with all that new profit.

# Two Methods of Accounting: Cash and Accrual Accounting Methods

There are two methods for accounting: cash and accrual accounting. As a small business owner, you have the option of choosing between these two methods.

## Cash method

For a small business owner, the cash method is the preferred because income is not income until cash or checks are received, and expenses are not counted until they are paid.

However, cash accounting can incorrectly reflect your revenue. For example, if you have a lot of business expenses but bring in a small amount of revenue in specific a period, it will look like you are losing money when that may not necessarily be true. If you bring in a large amount of revenue in a small period of time when you do not have many expenses to pay, this form of accounting may mislead you into believing you are making more money than you actually are.

## Accrual accounting

The accrual method gives you real-time financial data by recognizing when services are rendered and an expense when the business is obligated to pay it. In this form of accounting, income and expenses are matched to provide a proper view of your revenue. Using this system is easier with the latest accounting software packages that simplify the accrual accounting process. If you choose to move from the cash system to accrual accounting, this can be as simple as checking a box in your accounting software.

# PART THREE

# Expanding Your Business; Getting More Clients; Hiring Employees

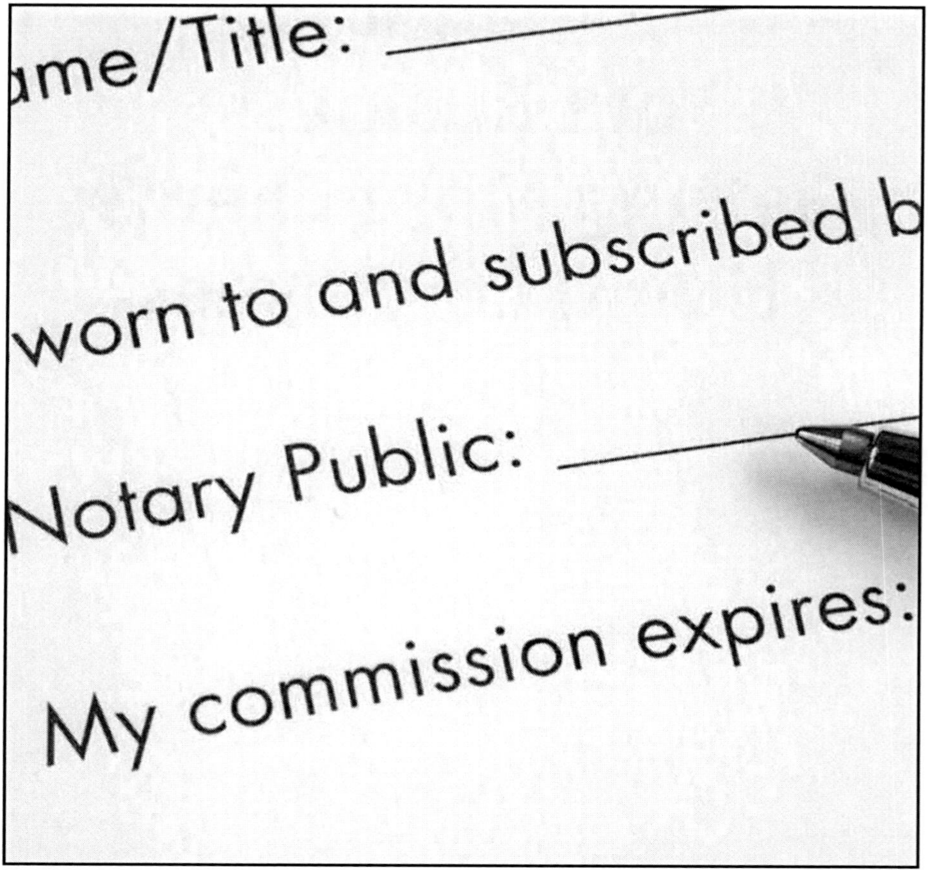
ame/Title:
worn to and subscribed b
Notary Public:
My commission expires:

CHAPTER 10:

# Marketing

*Y*our marketing plan, which is typically a large portion of your overall business plan, is the written plan you have for attracting the right clients to your notary business. Creating a winning marketing plan requires you to conduct some research on current and potential customers to fully understand whom your customers are, how they feel, and how they think. Then, the marketing plan consists of all of the advertising and marketing strategies you have to carry out to land them as clients. It is a study of your target market: who is buying, why they are buying, and how you will surpass the competition and get the market to buy from you.

Complete the marketing plan worksheet to help you start creating a picture of your customers.

## Marketing Plan Worksheet

Who are your current and potential customers?

_____

_____

Who are your competitors?

_____

_____

How can you compete in this market?

_____

_____

What are your strengths and weaknesses in comparison to competitors?

_____

_____

What can you do better than your competitors?

_____

_____

Are there any governmental or legal factors affecting your business?

_____

_____

What advantages does your service have over the competition?

_____

_____

What is your pricing strategy?

_____

_____

Is your pricing in line with your image?

_____

_____

Do your prices properly cover costs?

_____

_____

What types of promotion will you use? (Television, radio, direct mail, personal contacts, newspaper, magazines, Yellow Pages, billboard, Internet, classifieds, and trade associations.)

_____

_____

# Develop Your Logo

The logo is a visual symbol of your business and your brand. There are many different things to consider when choosing a logo or having one designed for you. You probably will want to keep it graphically simple, so it can be enlarged or made smaller, yet remain easily recognizable. A professional graphic designer may be helpful in preparing the symbol for use in multiple formats. It should look as good on a billboard as it does on your truck, an invoice statement, or your business cards.

You also will want to think ahead to the cost of reproducing your logo. Ideally, it will look good in black and white as well as in color, because color printing costs more, and you may want to conserve costs at some point. If it renders well in black and gray shading, it will deliver that much more of a punch when you can afford to print it in color.

The combined effect of your values statement, mission statement, vision, and position statement, plus your definition of market, your business name, and your logo will become, over time, the foundation of your brand. Your unique "business personality" will be presented to the target market through business cards, fliers, brochures, online ad media, the Yellow Pages, and possibly newspaper, radio, or

TV advertising. If you develop unified themes and are consistent in presenting your business message and image, your brand will grow with you as your customer list increases. People will know who you are and what you represent. That consistent, positive message will greatly increase your chances for profits and long-term success.

# Business Cards

Business cards are a necessity in a notary business. A simple, clear design with your logo, name, phone number, and website is adequate. Hand them out everywhere. Pin them up on bulletin boards. Have them handy whenever you are in a public place, at a trade show, in the home improvement store, or wherever people gather. Prepare your elevator speech (a 30-second description of your business) and be ready to deliver that speech, with a card, at every opportunity. The more people know who you are and what you do, the more business you will get.

# Using Social Media and Networking

Social networking is one of the latest forms of marketing. The main objective is to allow members who have the same interest to interact and exchange information. Many small businesses find social networking to be a great way to build and grow, especially in tough economic times when advertising budgets are low. Instead of paying for costly advertising, you can use social media to share information through word of mouth and websites that generally are free to use.

Social media networking refers to an online community or group of users where people can connect and communicate. The format may vary from one network to another, but communication takes place using blogs, e-mail, instant messaging, forums, video, or chat rooms. Social networking connects people across the world in the privacy of their own homes, and the networking sites are usually free and instantaneous. People can easily stay in touch with current customers, seek out past customers, or establish new relationships with customers and potential referral sources of business. Some of the thousands of social networking sites are primarily for social use, and others are for business networking.

## How it helps

Members of social networking sites are numerous, which creates an excellent opportunity for an individual to expand and promote a business without having to pay for advertising. With social networking, you can build an image and develop your customer base. To increase website traffic, many site owners leverage the value social networking sites have in drawing new customers. The following are some ideas on how to use social networking sites to generate website traffic:

- ▶ Link from your website to your social network profile.
- ▶ Use social bookmarking to increase your website's exposure on social networking sites.
- ▶ Create and share videos and photos on Flickr® and YouTube® describing your business, products, and services.
- ▶ Use social networking forums to promote your business, website, and blog.
- ▶ Promote your business through your profile, with links to your home page.

## Popular social networking sites

With the popularity of Internet use, social websites have become a must, as this is the best and the easiest way for people to get connected with each other and stay in touch.

**Orkut** is a popular social networking site owned by Google. This social networking site has millions of users; 63 percent of Orkut traffic originates from Brazil, followed by India with 19.2 percent. Like other sites such as Facebook®, Orkut permits the creation of groups known as "communities" based on a designated subject and allows other people to join the communities.

**Facebook** is the leading social networking site, with more than 500 million active users at the time of publication. Initially, Facebook was set up to connect university students, but over time, the site became available publicly, and its popularity exploded. Facebook users include people of all ages and backgrounds. On Facebook, it is extremely easy to add friends, send messages, and create communities or event invitations.

**YouTube®** is another social networking site owned by Google. To become a member of YouTube, go to the "Signup" page, choose a username and password, enter your information, and click the "Signup" button. YouTube is the largest video sharing network site in the world, and it is a great place to do video marketing.

**Digg™** is a place to unearth and share content retrieved anywhere on the Web. Digg is unique compared to other social networking sites because it allows you to directly network with people. Once a post is submitted, it appears on a list in the selected category. From there, members vote on the topic, so it can gain or fall in ranking. Digg is technically a "social bookmarking" site, which is a way to share, organize, and search bookmarks of Web pages or articles in an online, public forum instead of simply on browsers. Many social bookmarking sites allow users to vote on or recommend bookmarks, which allows content to grow more popular and be seen by a wider range of people the higher it is ranked. You submit your content to Digg, and other Digg users review and rate it. If it ranks high enough, your content may appear on the Digg homepage, which gets thousands of visitors a day, potentially driving tons of traffic to your website or blog.

**Twitter™** is different from other social networking sites, and Twitter's popularity has grown at an amazing rate. Twitter allows users to broadcast short messages — in Twitter's case 140 characters or fewer — to other users. With Twitter, you can let your followers know what you are doing with your business or share relevant information, when you sign up with Twitter, you can post and receive messages (known as a "tweet") with your Twitter™ account, and the site sends your tweets out to subscribers. In turn, you receive all the messages sent from those you wish to follow, including customers, colleagues, and referral sources.

## Popular business networking sites

The following sites offer businesses opportunities to network with other business owners.

- ▶ **Biznik® (www.biznik.com):** Its tagline: "Business networking that doesn't suck." Geared directly to entrepreneurs and business owners, with a number of different communities.

- ▶ **Ecademy (www.ecademy.com):** Provides extra tools to build your business, such as networking events, webinars on online topics, and the ability to locate members with specific knowledge.

- ▶ **Fast Pitch (www.fastpitchnetworking.com):** Reports it is growing faster than any other social network for professionals. Set up your own profile page, and network with other businesspeople.

- ▶ **Konnects® (www.konnects.com):** Gives each member a profile page. Join communities, meet other members, and network with professionals with similar interests.

- ▶ **LinkedIn® (www.linkedin.com):** Connect and network with others in your field who can use your abilities and/or services.

- ▶ **StartupNation® (www.startupnation.com):** Active forums with a wide variety of subjects for businesses.

- ▶ **StumbleUpon (www.stumbleupon.com):** Post any information of value and interest to others.

▶ **Upspring™ (www.upspring.com):** Increase exposure and attract more customers. Sign up free, get a profile page, find and join groups, and increase your networking activities.

▶ **Xing (www.xing.com):** An active group of professionals looking for ways to network with people of interest.

# Targeting Your Market

The key to increasing profits for your notary business is to discover who needs your notary services. Learn customer demographics and benefits they are seeking; focus on customer needs that your notary services can fulfill.

Once you understand who your customers are, you can offer the right notary services, but you can also effectively market the services in a manner that reaches the intended audience. Even when you build a regular client list and feel safe and content, be aware of other audiences or other ways you may be able to diversify or deepen current relationships. Check out title companies, medical-related industries, real estate, school, mortgage and other loan providers, and insurance companies, among others to identify notary business opportunities.

Another way to promote your new business venture is to network with people in your community and other notaries in your area. A good network can help you market and promote your business. Invest time and energy in cultivating people in the right places to build a continuous stream of business.

# Sales and Marketing Techniques

Sales and marketing are two different strategies, yet are used to accomplish the same goal — increase revenue. This is not to say that some sales strategies and techniques are not similar or the same as some marketing techniques. After all, the result is the same: to expose a service to the biggest group of people that can benefit from the service.

In sales, seven steps exist to get customers to purchase a service. The seven steps include:

1. **Preparation.** The preparation process is a step that should be taken well before you take any other steps in selling. This includes researching the market you are attempting to sell to and knowing your service. Many notary business owners begin sales and marketing techniques before they gain a full understanding of the service they are trying to pass along to public.

2. **Introduction.** How you present yourself when trying to get the sale is very important. This includes being confident in what your service will do for its customers and not being afraid to let them know more about your services.

3. **Questioning.** Questioning is where you find out from the customer exactly what he or she needs from the service. Many individuals are not always open to releasing all of their information or their reasoning for wanting to purchase something. Determining the customer's need for the notary service helps you as the business owner to better explain the features and benefits of the service.

4. **Presentation.** How you present your notary service offering to your target market can set you apart from the competition. What can you offer your potential customer? What will captivate them? Why will they keep coming back to you?

5. **Negotiation.** Though your presentation is what may win the customer over, if there are others offering the same service, you may have to negotiate to reel your potential customers in. Negotiations most often begin when the prospective customer is deciding whether to use your service; this is the time to take steps to ensure you are the person they buy the notary service from.

6. **Close the sale.** This is where you seal the deal and ensure customer satisfaction. Are they happy with the service you are providing? Do they wish they had taken their money and business somewhere else? Remember, every time you sell your service, you are advertising. People talk about the services they purchase with their friends, family, and just about anyone who will listen, whether the outcome is good or bad. Following steps to ensure your customers are happy generates positive word-of-mouth advertising.

7. **Follow-up and fulfillment.** Were you able to provide customers the exact service they wanted? Did they need anything from you after that? Are they happy with what they received? These are all questions you need to ask to make sure your service is the best out there.

Marketing techniques and sales techniques go hand-in-hand. The sales techniques help get you the sale, but the marketing techniques are what land the customers on your doorstep to allow you to implement the sales steps. Marketing, like sales, requires a great deal of thought and preparation. You need to research exactly how you intend to market your services, and there is a multitude of ways to do so.

One of the ways is through networking. Networking can be done face-to-face, within personal groups, within just a niche group (those that the product or service was designed for), or even through communications, such as bulletin boards and websites.

Another strategy in marketing is putting the word out in print. This can be accomplished by writing press releases, putting ads in newspapers, or having advertisements published on the Internet. Any advertising you distribute allows the public to see what services you have to offer. Take it a step further, and incorporate media relations into your marketing plan. Make the media aware that you are an expert in the notary field.

With a notary business, just like any other business, in order for individuals to use your service, they must know that you are offering it. This is where marketing and sales techniques become very useful. You can have a product and/or service that everyone wants and even needs desperately; however, no one will be knocking down your door to use your services if they do not realize you provide those services.

## *Word-of-mouth marketing*

Optimal customer satisfaction is achieved by providing punctual, cautious, and thorough notary services. This helps you build a good reputation and helps you with the next stage of publicity, advertising through word of mouth. Word-of-mouth advertising is one of the best and most effective marketing tools available. If you want to focus on word-of-mouth advertising strategies, the best way to do this is to make sure each person who takes part in your service is satisfied. Unfortunately, individuals most often speak about their bad experiences rather than their good experiences. However, if you wow your customers with your services, they are sure to tell others, who in turn will remember your name when they are looking for a notary.

You can request satisfied clients to spread the word based on the excellent service you have provided them. One great marketing strategy is to offer a word-of-mouth referral bonus. Offer individuals who refer others to your business a discount on future services. If people are pleased with what they received from you, they are more likely to think about you the next time they need the same or a similar service. Offering them another reason to come back can give you a great way to drum up new business and retain your current customers. Do not be afraid to ask for referrals. If you know that someone is pleased with the services you provided, let them know you appreciate them telling others about your service.

As your business grows, your marketing techniques can grow too. Diversify and increase your marketing slowly and as your business needs it. It is important to make the most of each marketing technique and strategy you implement, so that it is not a waste of your time or money.

# Developing a Mind-set for Marketing

Marketing is a skill you have to perfect. It works for each business differently. For some notaries, the first notary client comes easily, while others struggle to land the first piece of business. No business is built overnight; so do not get discouraged when testing out different ways to market your business.

It is not unheard of to spend 25 to 50 percent of your time marketing your notary services, which means being proactive in selling your services, advertising, and promoting your new business. Clients do not magically appear, but once you start attracting clients, more clients seek your services through word-of-mouth advertising and the other marketing efforts you implement.

The first thing to think about to begin creating a marketing mind-set is to decide what you want for your business. Are you interested in working with legal papers to notarize, to perform weddings, or to oversee real estate transactions? Once you decide the avenue of business you want to pursue, you have a starting point for your marketing mind-set. After you decide what clients you want to bring in to your business, you need to think from their point of view. What can you do to change your business so your target clients will feel most at home and want to return?

The next step to developing a marketing mind-set is to change what you can about your business so it gives your clients the most pleasant experience possible. Some things to improve upon could include your work values, your business intentions, or being more creative in your business.

Another aspect to a marketing mind-set is realizing it takes advertising and marketing your business in different ways to bring in new customers. The best way to bring people into a business is to create an awareness of your business in your market. A successful advertising campaign brings customers into your business and brings awareness to the services you are offering.

When devising a marketing plan, take into account your strengths, opportunities, and the demographics of your area. Just as your business plan forecasts any problems and the solutions to those problems, your marketing plan does the same. Target those weaknesses in the beginning; create solutions; and be proactive. Understand external threats, such as competition and economic factors. How can you surpass the competition? What can you do economically to keep your business moving forward? The core of your marketing strategy — namely, your services and media campaign — is to exceed what your competition may have already done. Then use your readily available marketing tools to bring clients into your fold.

Above all else, understand that marketing has to become second nature in your everyday business regimen. Weave your business marketing tasks into all of the daily tasks you have to complete every day for your business. If you start to neglect your marketing on a regular basis, you may lose clients and miss opportunities, which only hurts your business and income growth. In a challenging economy, it is more important than ever to be the company that offers a great price, reliability, and excellent customer service. However, without a regular marketing strategy, your existing and potential customers may find themselves interested in your competitor's latest offerings.

# Attracting the Next Client

Even in this digital age and during these times of electronic messaging and digital signatures, most binding agreements need a notarized signature. This need is the reason most notaries develop business plans based on their ability to attract new business regularly.

When it comes to your clients, it is important to realize the importance of target marketing. This is important because only a portion of the population will need your services. By carefully selecting your demographic audience with your marketing campaign, your marketing becomes more productive.

Successful signature service companies rely on more than the ability to perform a niche service. What makes companies profitable is an ability to attract and retain new clients. The notary can benefit from continued customer growth and the attraction of more revenue. Customers need you right now, but the question is, do they know how to find you?

Marketing is how you get your information to consumers who need your service. You have to be aggressive; you are not the only notary out there. To be successful, you must do cold calling, e-mailing, faxing, and be sure to follow up with the people you contact.

Knowing where your clients look for your service helps you get your message there. Matching your marketing messages with the right place brings immediate and future new clients to your notary business. For example, if your target market is real estate agents, talk to some local real estate agents and find out what process they go through when trying to find a notary. The more your audience receives exposure to your business, the better your chances are of landing their business.

When you are developing marketing strategies, remember the four P's of marketing: price, product, promotion, and place. With the right message and delivery of the message, you can begin to drive new clients to your door. Your success is up to you. A great way to build a business is with marketing, and the quickest way to failure is ignoring it. Do not become so comfortable or fatigued with your marketing plan than you neglect to nurture and use it. A marketing plan is not something you create and then never change it. Re-evaluate your marketing plan at least once or twice a year to study which marketing techniques have produced positive and negative results. Evaluating this information allows you to mimic the successes and modify failures for a better future outcome

The following seven marketing tips provide easy, inexpensive ways to attract new clients and increase profits:

1. **Advertise wisely.** Work with the money you have and include a special offer or tracking code in your advertising to make it easier for potential clients to respond and for you to track where your business is coming from.

2. **Provide an inexpensive version.** Be creative with the services you offer and create special deals and service packages for clients, especially your regular clients.

3. **Provide a premium version.** Not all customers are looking for inexpensive services; many clients only want the best, so offer a more deluxe service or combine services that you are able to offer.

4. **Try unorthodox marketing methods.** Create your best ad, have it printed on a postcard, mail it out to potential clients in your target market, or advertise on the place mat of a local restaurant frequented by your audience.

5. **Smaller print ads.** Choose the words for your ads carefully.

6. **Promote and advertise with other small businesses.** Work with other small businesses to publicize your services to your customers in exchange for their publicizing your services to their customers.

7. **Take advantage of your customer base.** Your customers know and trust you. Do not overlook your existing customer base; pay attention to your valued customers, and announce new services to these customers before you announce them to the general market.

The mainstay of your notary businesses is the client, so you must reach out to new customers and continue to satisfy existing customers in ways that generate profits for your notary business. Again, to do this, a business must make competent and valuable use of its marketing tools.

Use of established sales and marketing strategies will help a notary business venture grow, thrive, and reap a profit in a competitive industry.

# Generating Publicity for Your Notary Business

Aside from mastering notary public skills, you also need proper publicity in order to have an advantage over other notaries.

To draw more recognition to your business, try attending high-profile events, possibly even being a sponsor of a special event, such as a real estate law seminar. Networking is another way to publicize your business. One way of doing this is attending meetings for your local chamber of commerce as a guest or keynote speaker on a topic that relates to your business and is relevant to the audience (such as identity theft). This could help you get connections with other businesses.

One of the key programs that will help to boost your business and subscriber list while increasing credibility is publicity. Publicity is a low-cost, effective way to reach your target audience. The purpose of publicity for a notary business is:

▶ To inform potential clients and referral sources about you, your company, your services, and how you can help them

▶ To educate the media and potential clients in order to shape attitudes and behaviors and change perceptions about the industry

▶ To effectively communicate your marketing messages

# *Public relations*

Public relations (PR) is one of the easiest, most cost-effective ways to promote who you are and what you do so you can get more clients and more sales for your business. PR builds credibility and visibility that helps you gain new clients and can increase your income. Public relations is the art of building favorable and profitable interest in you, your business, or your service by creating a "buzz" in the marketplace. PR gets your message across and tells others about you, what you do, and why it is important to them. Public relations lends you credibility and builds your reputation from a third-party point of view; therefore, it is often more valuable than advertising alone. PR is effective because it:

▶ Creates awareness of your brand

▶ Communicates the benefits of your services

▶ Positions you as an expert

▶ Generates sales and leads

PR is usually free and lends more credibility to your claims than paid advertisements. It is the most cost-effective way to generate interest about your notary business and reach existing and potential clients. When people read about you in the media from a journalist or hear about you on the radio, you get instant third-party validation and receive positioning as an expert in your field. A paid advertisement placed in a publication can cost you tens of thousands of dollars each time it is run, but a well-placed article is much more cost effective and adds value to your business.

Trade publications have a number of subscribers, and most have thousands of readers, each of whom is a prospect that may need the services your notary business offers. At the very least, the readers likely know someone who needs the services you provide. In addition, this positions you as an expert, which produces a premium price for your services because people are more willing to pay more for your expertise. This often removes price as an obstacle to overcome in the process of attracting new clients. PR also levels the playing field and allows small businesses to appear larger than they are and compete on the same level as larger businesses.

PR helps you attract qualified prospects and leads. The more people know about you, the higher the level of trust it builds, which makes it more likely they will contact you and refer others to you. As an added bonus, current clients get the confirmation they need that your business is the best one with which to do business. Here is how to get started:

**Develop a media list:** A media list should include local and national outlets that will have an interest in covering your story. It is important to find individual reporters, journalists, and writers for the publication that would have an interest in covering your story. You will need to gather and maintain a PR contact list for these local journalists and publications, either by paying for these subscriptions or doing independent research online.

**Implement editorial calendars:** Most print publications publish a calendar — called an editorial calendar — outlining topics they will be covering throughout the year. Use the editorial calendars of your top media outlets to help you to develop story ideas for promoting your business. These lists are useful when pitching story ideas, so you can tie in your story with these topics. Also, monitor and identify publicity opportunities from journalists and lists such as Help a Reporter Out™ (**http://helpareporter.com**), Pitch Rate (**http://pitchrate.com**), and Reporter's Source (**www.reporterssource.com**). By responding to a reporter's source query, you are establishing yourself as an expert in your notary niche. Your credibility and reputation can only build if you are positively quoted in a news article.

**Write a pitch:** Your pitch should be personalized to the person you are pitching the story to. Mention similar stories they have covered, or point out why their readers would be interested in the story you have to tell. The pitch also should include an overview of the story and have the press release attached for more details.

To start, determine the top three local media outlets for newspaper, TV, and radio in the area where you run your notary business. Send press releases to specific journalists or editors, and follow up accordingly.

**Write a monthly press release.** You should send out one press release per month for special events, workshops, or webinars you are promoting. An easy strategy if you do not have something specific to promote for the month is to use your blog or monthly e-newsletter articles as a press release. This way, you leverage your writing and are able to use your content in multiple places and for multiple purposes.

When writing a press release for online media, the main goal is to get keywords picked up by search engines. A search engine-optimized (SEO) press release is geared toward specific keywords rather than a specific story idea. SEO press releases are written and used online in order to increase the amount of traffic you drive to your website. Keyword-focused press releases are generally distributed through wire services. Many companies — especially larger ones — are sending press releases through these online services for the primary purpose of driving traffic to their websites. Submit your monthly press releases to the top five online press release distribution sites, which include one paid service and four free services.

| ONLINE PRESS RELEASE DISTRIBUTION CHANNELS | |
|---|---|
| PRWeb.com | $80/release |
| I-newswire.com | Free |
| IdeaMarketers.com | Free |
| Free-press-release.com | Free |
| 24-7pressrelease.com | Free |

**Pitch to the media, and follow up frequently:** Once a month when you write the press release, pitch the story to the appropriate media outlets. Follow up with each media contact you have pitched the story to and make sure they received the information. Use the follow-up as an opportunity to see if they are interested in covering the story.

## Speaking opportunities

Speaking opportunities can be an excellent source for new prospects and sale conversions. You can use speaking opportunities to expand your reach and position yourself as an expert in your field. Off-site speaking engagements help you reach potential clients while simultaneously enforcing the establishment of your expertise. Some options include being a guest speaker for radio shows, webinars, and workshops — online or live.

Speaking engagements allow notaries to connect face-to-face with current and potential clients and referral sources. It provides the opportunity to showcase areas of expertise, schedule appointments with potential clients, and even close sales.

Have a system in place to gather the names and contact information of the attendees of the show or event where you are speaking. Run a contest to gather attendee names, e-mail addresses, and telephone numbers; this allows you to build your list of leads and provides you with the opportunity to follow up with those leads to try to convert them into clients.

Speaking engagements are also prime locations for selling services on the spot. Run a show or speaking engagement special so if a prospect becomes a client at the show, they receive a special discount or bonus offer.

## *Write a book*

The purpose of writing a book is to promote your expertise. You can write and self-publish a book using a print-on-demand website online (such as **www.lulu.com** or **www.cafepress.com**) on a topic that is hot in your industry. You can sell the book on notary websites and at public speaking engagements. Book sales are another lead-gathering tactic, where you can then communicate with book buyers to convert them into a notary client.

## CASE STUDY: JUST BE GENUINE

Candice Moore
Notary Signing Agent and Paralegal

Candice Moore, a notary in the state of New York, embarked on her career as a notary 11 years ago. Moore began her career as a paralegal and becoming a notary was a benefit to her career. She now notarizes on average five to ten documents a day as varied as affidavits, authorizations, legal documents for divorces, family petitions, and real estate documents, to name a few.

Moore has found that being self-employed was one of the best choices she could make in life. She found the transition of going to her job, doing her work, and coming home to be difficult at first, but quickly developed her own routine for working at home to be successful. She understands that there are days when she does have to work after-hours and even some weekends, but Moore has thrived on her routine. She is one of those people who tend to be more successful as their own boss with her own notary business and enjoys everything that her job brings into her life, the freedom she now has, and the opportunity to make more money. It is all part of being your own boss.

Marketing, as Moore explained, was a new skill she had to learn. However, she finds using the classifieds and the Internet (mostly Craigslist) to be the best sources of work for her. She realized early on that it was more than just marketing. It was determination and getting her name out there that has brought her success in the notary field. She discovered that finding unique, niche services are an excellent way to reach new and valued customers — for example, being a mobile notary where she is able to provide in-home services.

Candice's advice to the aspiring notary: "Just be genuine!"

# Developing an Online Presence

Maintaining a website for your business is crucial. Most people searching for a business in their area will begin with an Internet search. Give your clients information and a reason to use your services. The following section outlines the basic components of a website, how to hire a Web designer, how to use a website for your business, and the fundamentals of search engine optimization (SEO). Remember to update your site with fresh information, new pictures, updated contact information, and new design features on a constant basis.

## Website Design Fundamentals

There are two basic components to a website: the Web pages and the content each page contains (images, copy, and other information displayed on the pages). Your website can be as small as one page or include multiple pages. The home page is the main page of the site that visitors land on when they type in your website domain address. From your home page, visitors can easily navigate to other pages on your site. All websites should be dynamic, so even after an initial design is created and published, further maintenance, updating, and revisions are required. The most challenging part of creating a website is developing a blueprint for how you want your site organized, what pages it will contain, how content will be organized, and how your pages will be laid out in relation to others as you design your navigation and page relationships. Design your pages individually, formulate what each page should include, and then you can flesh out the actual content and site design later. You can do this work on a piece of paper or even with sticky notes on the wall to help you visualize the layout.

One of the first things to recognize when building a website is that you will either need some type of software program or you will have to learn HTML coding and build your site from the ground up. For those determined to learn all of the coding necessary to build and maintain a website, we will explore these options later in the book, as well as look at a variety of software options to help you with your design goals. Starting out with the availability of adding interactive content and items to your website is the best route to take, because even if you do not plan to use them in the beginning, you most likely will use them down the road. When approaching your website design, it is usually best to keep colors and fonts at a basic level.

## Four main components of a website

1.  **Domain name:** This name is registered, corresponds with where your website is physically located on a Web server, and is used for your e-mail accounts.

2.  **Web hosting:** This is the physical "storage" of your website, so when someone types in your domain name, the pages you have created appear.

3.  **Web pages:** These are the Web pages you create and publish to your Web server. You can create Web pages with programs such as Microsoft Office

FrontPage, Microsoft Expression® Web, Adobe® Dreamweaver® CS4, and many other applications, including free design applications.

4. **Optional items:** These might include shopping carts, forms, or databases. Although none of these are required for websites, you will find your needs may change over time, so keep that in mind during the planning process.

## Hire a Web designer

A professional website can cost a couple hundred or tens of thousands of dollars, depending on the complexity of the site. Most notary sites are basic informational sites that fall in the lower half of the cost category. This money buys layout, design, copywriting, programming, and the first year of hosting. Keep these suggestions in mind if you decide to hire a Web designer:

▶ You can find a Web designer online.

   ◆ Search for "Web design [your city name]," or "insert business type Web design" for people with experience designing insert type service sites.

▶ Look at insert type business sites.

   ◆ When you find a design you like, contact the webmaster. The webmaster is usually listed at the bottom of the home page.

   ◆ Visit sites and take notes about what you like and what you do not like.

▶ Review designers' portfolios and samples.

   ◆ Do they grab your attention?

   ◆ Do the links work and do the graphics load quickly?

   ◆ Is it immediately obvious what the site is promoting?

# Domain Names

Your domain name is the address every site visitor types in to visit your website, and it is critical that you choose a good domain name and use a reputable provider to host it. You can purchase your domain name from dozens of companies. Your domain name should uniquely identify your business. The general rule is that the shorter the domain name, the better, and it should be relevant to your company name and services.

If you already have an established corporate name or identity, you should try to base your domain name on that corporate identity to allow customers to identify your company name with your domain name. For example, Atlantic Publishing Group, Inc., uses the domain name **www.atlantic-pub.com**. It is also recommended that you secure any similar domain names, the main reason being to protect your identity from others who may use a very similar sounding or identical domain name, with a different extension. Using the example above, you would also want to purchase **www.atlanticpub.com**, **www.atlanticpub.net**, and **www.atlanticpublishing.com**. Your primary domain name should be the domain name that is "hosted," while others may be parked at no additional cost and pointed to the main domain name URL. This way, you only pay for one hosted domain name but use many domain names on the Internet, all directing site visitors to your main hosted site.

It is important that you name your website after your domain name. The primary reason for this is so that people know your website and business by name. CNN stands for Cable News Network, but no one calls it that. CNN is known as CNN, and the domain name is CNN.com. Your domain name should easily relate to your company name so your "brand" or company name can be easily recognized or memorized.

Many professional Web designers recommend using keywords in your domain name rather than your company name. For example, the

**www.strugglingteens.com** domain name specifically targets the industry of private schools and programs by using the keywords "struggling teens." Therefore, when you type the keywords "struggling teens" into the Google and Yahoo! search engines, this website pops up in the No. 1 spot under the paid ads. Your domain name may have relevance in how some search engines rank your website, so embedding keywords (such as notary) into your domain name may help you achieve better search engine success. Another option is to purchase domains names identifying your business and those using keywords. Put your website files on the domain name with the keywords and redirect the domain names with the company name to the keywords domain name. This will allow you to market the domain name with your company name, which helps with branding and to get the benefits of having the actual website located under a domain name with keywords.

A domain name should not be extremely long; this is going to be the URL address for your website, and you want it to be short enough to be memorable. Although some people may bookmark your page in their Internet browser, just as many, if not more, will not. You could lose valuable traffic if your website address is too long. If you are determined to have a long URL address, hyphenating the words can make it easier.

You can check the availability of a domain name by using services such as Go Daddy (**www.godaddy.com**).

# Search Engine Optimization — Explained

While designing your website, you will read and hear a great deal about search engine optimization (SEO). **Search engine optimization (SEO)** is a marketing tool used to increase a website's rank among search engines.

SEO involves developing your website in a way that will give you the maximum visibility with search engines. The more customers who see your services and information listed on Google, the greater the chance they will click on your business's link. The closer your listing is to the top of the first page, the more clicks you have the potential to gain. Understanding how SEO works is not difficult. Applying it to your site in a productive manner, however, takes considerable work. Website marketing has become very sophisticated due to increasing levels of available technology. With millions of websites competing for potential customers, it has become increasingly complex to ensure your website is found by interested buyers.

Internet professionals have their own ideas on how to achieve high rankings. Search engines are often called spiders, because they crawl across the Internet looking for morsels of information. In this case, search engines are searching for words and phrases, and they prefer the newest, most interesting ones they can find. These spiders, or search engines, hunt, retrieve, and collect information based on the keywords requested by users. They are searching for the most relevant results. Search engine spiders study the content of websites and rank content by hunting for specific phrases. They use two or more related words or phrases to garner the basic meaning of your page. Providing relevant, frequently updated copy with the right keywords and phrases helps attract these spiders to your site.

Fresh content is the key because search engines seek new content on a constant basis. If your content grows stale or you rarely add new copy, search engines will overlook your website. Your website's home page alone is not enough to keep the search engines happy. Blogs or extra pages with additional copy attached to your main website are required to rouse the interest of a search engine. Most important, you need to integrate the keywords or those special words pertaining to your notary service into your website design, copy, and videos. Use a different title and description with keywords on each page. Remember, the title of the page is the most important SEO factor. Also, do not forget to include a site map on your website. The search engine spiders cannot index pages if they are not available. Site maps help search engines understand the layout of your site. Using these keywords helps you "optimize" your website and gain positioning in the search engine pages.

## Overuse of SEO keywords and other banned tactics

Although using keywords on your site is necessary for SEO, overdoing it can have a detrimental effect on your rankings. When websites are stuffed with keywords, the copy becomes unintelligible, so search engines and customers know you are trying to scam the system. When this happens, the search engine spiders stop visiting your site, resulting in low rankings.

The recommended keyword density ranges from 3 to 7 percent per article. Anything more starts to look like keyword stuffing. It is even more important to have the correct density in the title, headings, and opening paragraphs. You can find keyword density tools online to help determine whether your keywords are within the correct range. If not, find synonyms, or rewrite the copy.

Hidden text is also a forbidden SEO tactic and occurs when the text and links are designed to be the same color as the background, such as white words on a white background. Search engines not only pass these over, but also may punish you for such practices. This tactic is similar to hidden links or doorway pages, which are written into websites exclusively to achieve high rankings. Duplicate pages with the same copy used repeatedly also are nixed and no longer acceptable. The search engines are just as stringent on the number of links per page, monitoring the number of both outbound and inbound links. There are also programs designed to measure your link density.

Another SEO turnoff is using small or unreadable type to fit more words into the design of the website. The biggest no-no in terms of keywords is one that not only disturbs the search engines, but also your visitors as well. This involves adding keywords to written text on your page that have nothing to do with the theme of the page. Keywords are important, but it is how the words are used that matters.

Unfortunately, the SEO process is becoming increasingly complex because Google and the other search engines continually change their search parameters. Because of this, many business owners use qualified SEO experts who are familiar with the latest changes. These professionals are hired to deliver SEO results by ensuring the websites are readily seen by potential customers. Also, check with your website host, which may offer this service at an additional cost. Hiring an SEO expert can be costly, so you need to decide how much of your marketing budget will be spent on optimization. Consider taking on this responsibility yourself, and put aside a couple hours each day to ensure your website is getting the best placement. The more you are committed to the process, the better the results will be.

## *Some additional SEO tips*

There are some basic things you can do to increase the chances the search engines pick up your copy including:

- ▶ Commit yourself to SEO. It is something that you need to work on at least once a day. The more you are committed to the process, the better the results will be.

- ▶ Make SEO part of your marketing plan. You need clear SEO goals, an outline of how you expect to achieve them, and at what cost.

- ▶ Be patient. After your website goes up, it will take at least two to three months of your hard editorial work to get the rankings you want in the search engines. The smaller and newer your business, the more difficult it becomes. That is why you want to work on this continually.

▶ Put at least a couple of topics of interest, which are original and not copied from elsewhere, on your website every week using your keywords. The search engines like new material. This also gives you an opportunity to write about other information on your services.

▶ Build your website with a number of different pages and more copy. This gives you additional opportunities with the search engines. On each page you have online, there is another way to use keywords that will be searched and will reach specific potential customers. You can end up with hundreds of content pages, each one able to be indexed by the search engines. Use the keywords that you find are most searched in your copy.

▶ Keep quality in mind at all times. You want strong editorial content that will be of interest to your readers and the search engines.

▶ Construct an interesting website, and always strive to make it better. That means adding content of interest to your main buyers.

▶ Do not forget your site map. Those spiders cannot index pages that cannot be crawled. Your site map will help the search engines understand the layout of your pages.

▶ When you decide on your URL, think SEO. Keywords in your website name are quite useful.

▶ Use a different, pertinent title and meta-description on each page. Remember that the title of the page is the most important SEO factor. The meta-description tag will not help in your ranking, but will appear in your listing and encourage people interested in the topic to look for more.

▶ Make your copy interesting for your primary readers. They are the ones who will be coming to your site and buying your services repeatedly.

▶ You want copy that is different from other websites, which can be difficult to accomplish for some. Put some time into your service descriptions, and stay away from the boilerplate information provided by most notaries. If you weave your keywords into your descriptions, you will be ahead of the pack.

▸ Use keywords as anchor text when linking internally. These tell the search engines what the page is all about.

# Meta Tag Definition and Implementation

Meta tags are a key part of the overall SEO program that you need to implement for your website. Controversy remains surrounding the use of meta tags and whether their inclusion on websites truly impacts search engine rankings, but they are still an integral part of a sound SEO plan, and some search engines do use these tags in their indexing process. You will find conflicting guidance on whether Google uses or ignores meta tags. Your site will compete against thousands or more of other websites. These other sites potentially can promote similar products using similar keywords and using other SEO techniques to attain that top search engine ranking. Using meta tags may offer a degree of control, letting you influence how search engines will index your Web pages. However, there is no guarantee of top rankings on crawler-based search engines.

Only use keywords and phrases that you have added within the material contained on your Web pages. Keep in mind to use the plural forms of keywords so all forms of words will show up in a search. Implementing words that are intentionally spelled wrong may increase the chances of people locating your site.

Avoid repeated instances of keywords and phrases in a meta keyword tag. Area-specific products or services should be noted in your meta-keyword tag (e.g., New York City, NY).

The HTML encoding for each head section on a website contains meta tags. In order to view the head of the page, you need to look at the HTML code. For

Internet Explorer® users, use the "View" menu on your toolbar and choose the "Source" option to figure out the origin of any website. When using a design tool, such as Adobe Dreamweaver CS4, Microsoft SharePoint® Designer 2007, or Microsoft Expression Web Designer, make sure you are in the HTML view when you need to modify your source code. Other editing tools for this purpose include Notepad and TextEdit.

## *Keyword density*

Keyword density is another factor that affects your search engine results. Keyword density is defined as the number of times a keyword or key phrase is found within the text of a single Web page. This typically is ranked in relative order to the other words on the page, so each word is compared to each word. The number of times a single word or phrase is used in contrast to all the other words factors into the total density of that particular word or phrase. When writing Web page content, consider increased keyword density as a goal to achieve. Balance this against keyword stuffing (adding excessive keywords to a page) and remember, it is relative to other page content, so five keywords in a 100-word page are less dense than five keywords in a 50-word page.

# Building a Website

If you are serious about your business, then you need a web presence to market your business online. A successful website is able to generate a high volume of traffic almost effortlessly and automatically. Other qualities that characterize a well-designed website include user-friendly navigation, high-quality content, search engine optimization, and the ability to easily upload information. Although it is important for your business to have its own site, not everyone has the technical know-how to build a website. Other qualities that characterize a well-designed website would include user-friendly navigability, clear and high-quality content, search engine optimization, and easy uploading even in outdated computers and software.

You should provide your notary qualifications and credentials in detail. You can also list the laws and rules for best practices and the detailed code of ethical and professional conduct to demonstrate to the online viewer that you know what you are doing. The website must carry a disclaimer that you are only authorized to serve as an independent witness to the signing of documents and to authenticate documents. You are not a lawyer and cannot give legal advice. You can include your website in online business directories to gain further exposure. It is important for you to have an online presence. Even if it is up to potential clients to find out how to contact you, it is still important. It is cheaper than creating a brochure or a print advertisement. You could create your own website at one of the many blogging websites — all free.

This all sounds easy. You would think that with the help of a book and a little practice, you would be able to build your own site successfully. Some people will be able to use a book and a little practice to build their own site. But if you cannot create your website or are finding it too difficult, you can hire a professional Web designer. Try using referrals and visit the websites of various web design companies to find a designer. Here are a few steps that would help you get your dream website up and running.

Your notary website may be a potential client's first impression of you and your business, so spend time planning a clear outline of the impression you want your website to make. Create a comprehensive list of the information you want to add on your site. Once you have an outline of all the information you want to include, write content for each area. Choose graphics and photographs that are representative of the notary business and the impression you want to make on visitors. Match the graphic items with the text. If you cannot afford to hire a Web designer, the following are free or inexpensive Web design tools and sites you can use to go it alone:

▶ Homestead® (**www.homestead.com**): Choose your design, customize, and publish your own site. $4.99/month after a 30-day free trial.

▶ Microsoft Small Business: Building free professional business. Can choose your domain, add e-mail, and store/share documents

▶ Wix® (**www.Wix.com**): Free Flash® website creation. Can choose pro Wix designers to make your site. Flash photo galleries and professional designs available

▶ Web (**www.web.com®**): Provides site design, search engine optimization, and website hosting. Enables users to attract customers and sell products online

If you can afford to hire a Web designer, the next step then is finding the right professional. Decide first how much of your marketing budget you can invest in a business website before you start searching for a web designer. Keep in mind having your website designed could cost anywhere between $100 and $10,000. Another thing you need to consider is what you pay for is what you get. The less money you pay for your website, the less professional it will likely look.

Choose a Web designer after doing your due diligence of checking credentials, reputation, and references. If your budget is limited, you may want to find a freelance graphic or Web designer, aiming for high quality with a reasonable price tag.

The next step is testing your website. Plan for about one month as testing time, and ask everyone you know to visit your site and give you feedback. Many times, parts of your site do not function the way you want it to, but without testing, you may not know, and a non-functioning website may send potential customers away to visit another notary's site. Once your testing period is over and everything is running properly, it is time for you to launch your site. Some effective ways to increase traffic to your site include adding forums and posting business-related content on Twitter and YouTube. Now, you are all set to drive traffic to your website and do business.

The marketing plan is really the action part of your business; you can take these steps proactively in order to promote the business, make people aware that the business exists, and find new clients. There are two sides to every marketing plan, which covers online and offline tactics you can use as a notary to attract the clients that fall into your target market and be hired by those clients. You can use the marketing plan as is to get started. The thing with marketing plans is that they are dynamic documents because after you implement the plan, you have to go back and evaluate the success or failure of your marketing tactics. Once you analyze the results, you can then tweak and adjust the marketing plan that needs to be implemented for the next six months to a year.

One important factor to keep in mind is that marketing a notary business is a process. You cannot conduct a marketing activity one time and then decide that it is a complete failure because you do not see immediate results. You must take consistent action in implementing your marketing strategies for at least six months to a year.

The first part of the marketing plan is the marketing strategy. For a notary business, three marketing strategies exist. Commit these three strategies to memory because every marketing activity covered in the remainder of the plan hinges on these three strategies.

1. Gather qualified leads and followers to grow your subscriber list and database.

2. Nurture the qualified leads and followers in your database by consistently getting in front of them in various ways with information about your notary services.

3. Convert the leads into clients and generate revenue by introducing them to your notary services.

# Marketing Foundation

Before you can start to implement and integrate the various marketing activities set forth in the marketing plan, you first have to build your marketing foundation. Building your marketing foundation includes putting together marketing pieces and collateral, which was discussed in detail in Chapter 10. Because the first half of the marketing plan covers the online activities you can partake in to attract clients, the notary business website needs to be up and fully functioning so that you have a venue to drive traffic to when marketing your notary services online.

To build the brand of the notary business, which tackles the first marketing strategy, there are a few implementation strategies to include as part of the website in order to grab the attention of your ideal client. Traffic should be driven to the website from a variety of venues, which will be discussed later in the plan. Driving traffic to the home page of the website will be an important first step to gathering leads and converting them into clients. It will set the stage for learning more about these prospects and then up-selling them into the next logical service level you offer that fits their needs.

By incorporating certain elements into your website design, you can increase the credibility of your notary website, allowing for the gathering of highly targeted leads that can be further qualified and turned into more revenue for the business. The following are elements your website should include:

**Entice with an irresistible free offer:** Offer an incentive to help capture information on the visitors to your website. An irresistible free offer may be a free downloadable report on a topic of interest to them. In exchange for the visitors to your site giving you their name and e-mail address, provide them something free. Capturing these leads is the key to building your database of prospective clients. If visitors to your site are interested in accepting your free gift in exchange for providing you with their information, then they are potential clients for your business — at least up front. The rest of your marketing activities help you further qualify these leads and eventually move them into client status.

**Further qualify subscribers:** As part of the subscription process, add a one-question survey to the free offer subscription. Use a question that directly relates to the challenges your clients may face. For example, a notary may ask, "What is your biggest question having documents notarized?" The point of the question is to find out what your prospects are thinking, seeking information about, or feeling. You can then use the information you gather to create solutions that cater directly to what clients and prospects are seeking.

**Ensure comprehensive branding:** Make sure that your branding is carried throughout all of your website pages, autoresponders, and other marketing collateral for consistency purposes. Use the same color schemes, font styles, layouts, and templates throughout all of your materials.

**Optimize your pages:** Use keywords in the copy of your website that prospective clients would use to search for the products or services your notary business offers; this is the basis of search engine optimization (SEO). Choose one or two keywords to focus on for each page of your site, and then scatter the keywords, phrase, and combinations of the phrase in the beginning, in the middle, and toward the end of your copy. Make sure that the copy is written to include the keywords so that text flows and sounds natural. You can use free keyword tools such as the Google AdWords™ Keyword Tool, or you can hire a professional keyword or SEO professional to help you come up with a list of keywords to include on the site.

If you provide services to a confined geographic area, be sure to include keywords that speak about the area you cover. You should also use the keywords in the page titles, headlines, and subheadings in the copy on each page.

# Internet Marketing and List-building

A growing business requires you to grow your existing database steadily by gathering highly targeted new leads. This creates the foundation for significant business growth and increased revenue for your notary business. Once you fill your database with the ideal prospects you seek, you can then work on selling them your fee-based products and services by communicating with them on a regular basis. Here are some ways to keep your clients up to date:

**E-newsletter:** Regularly publish an e-mail newsletter to create an automatic lead-capturing system online and as a communication tool for your existing database.

**Editorial calendar:** Create an editorial calendar to map out discussion topics for the next six weeks or so. Block out time on your calendar each week to create this content and post it on your blog. You can also use existing content you have — such as products, presentations, and reports — to break down and turn into blog posts. Each blog post should be approximately 200 to 400 words. The editorial calendar can also be used for creating e-newsletter articles and social media updates.

## Social media

Harnessing the power of social media outlets drives more targeted traffic to your website, which will drive more clients to your notary business. This provides you with the opportunity to communicate with your target market on a more regular basis and in different ways, and it can have a powerful and positive effect on growing your list and your notary business. Social media networks include Facebook, Twitter, LinkedIn, and YouTube. Each social media network works a bit differently, so you will need to familiarize yourself with each one. The following sections go into detail on how you can use each network as part of your social media marketing efforts. You can implement the following social media strategies:

## Facebook Fan Page

Create a Facebook Fan Page that speaks directly to your target markets and focuses on the geographic area of your business (if applicable). On the fan page for your business, you can also include an opt-in box for your free offer so visitors can immediately subscribe to your list and be taken to your website. To build your fan base, include a special announcement in your e-newsletter to drive traffic to the fan page. Be sure to include a link to your fan page in every piece of correspondence you have with your prospects and client. This way, you are creating a two-way street — driving traffic from social media to your website and vice versa. If you can gather video or audio testimonials from clients, these are also great ways to let your services speak for themselves. If not, then record case studies or scenarios where you can illustrate how your service helped a client gain success.

You can use the Facebook Fan Page in various ways, including sharing your blog posts with links to drive them directly to where the post sits on your site, posing questions to your audience in an effort to engage them and make it more of an interactive experience. This allows you to evaluate who your audience is on your fan page so you can then work on funneling them into the appropriate service level of your business. You can also integrate your Twitter account with your fan page so your updates get more exposure and even have a custom background created that matches your brand in addition to the sidebar information about your business. A dramatic or attractive background can boost interest for followers.

## Facebook profile

Because Facebook limits actual profiles to individuals, it is better practice to create a Facebook Fan Page or group for your notary business and integrate your personal Facebook page with your business's page. Use your personal profile page to talk about your professional relationship to the business, join relevant groups, and RSVP to events that connect to your target market. Join groups or become a fan of any professional organizations you belong to and any of your competitors. Also, integrate your Twitter account with your profile so that your updates get more exposure.

## Twitter

Twitter is another social media marketing tool you can use to promote your notary business online. Use Twitter to share information, products, and services related to your business. This helps position you as an expert resource for information without always trying to sell your products and services. Aim for 80 percent information sharing and 20 percent promotion. You can integrate your tweets with your blog posts and articles, which is a highly effective way to attract followers, and it permits you to communicate with your followers and drive them to your website. Almost all tweets should include a link to a specific blog article, product, or service on your website. Sharing helpful tips or information on Twitter has to be done within the 140 characters that Twitter allows for tweets. Make your tweets intriguing, and then send your followers somewhere they can get more information by including a link. Twitter allows you to share information, but your goal is to use it as a tool to drive traffic to your notary website — as is the goal with all of your social media marketing. Be sure to use the "shorten URL" feature on Twitter to keep the length of the URLs as short as possible; bitly™ (**http://bit.ly**) is a URL shortener that also tracks your links, giving you information on how active a certain post is.

Follow people you admire — authors, bloggers, e-zines you read, seminars you attend, or leaders in your field — as well as your competitors. Visit these profiles and their lists of followers to find people to follow that fit your target market. Consider having a custom background created that matches your brand in addition to the sidebar information about your business. A dramatic or attractive background can boost interest for followers.

## LinkedIn

LinkedIn is another online source for professionals, business owners, and entrepreneurs that can develop your notary services. Add a direct link to your website's home page in your profile so people can take advantage of your free offer right away. Your LinkedIn profile should connect to your blog for further exposure of your content. You can start connecting with individuals who are in related businesses. This is a great way to connect with possible joint venture partners, potential clients, and other referral sources. Also, look for people located in the geographic area your business covers, if applicable. This is a great way to connect with potential clients as well as referral sources.

LinkedIn provides a built-in application for gathering recommendations from clients you have worked with or other professionals on LinkedIn that you have done business with. Spend some time once per quarter gathering recommendations from your contacts. LinkedIn can be a very powerful tool, especially after you have connected with at least 500 other professionals. Even if you cannot get recommendations, you need to use LinkedIn as a tool to connect with your target audiences.

## YouTube

Create and use a free YouTube account to upload instructional videos that speak on a certain point of interest to your target audiences. You can also turn each of your written blog posts and/or e-newsletter articles into a video. You are providing just enough information to encourage your audience to gain more information by going to your website. These videos also can be added to your Facebook profile and fan page for additional exposure.

Remember, you want to be everywhere that your target audience is, and your target market is using these social media websites.

## *Blog*

Having an up-to-date blog is one of the primary ways people are going to find your notary business online because search engines look for updated content when determining page rank. Share your expertise about your business, industry, or niche in your blog posts. Then, integrate your blog with the social media sites (Facebook, LinkedIn, and Twitter) to help drive traffic to your site. Mix it up between longer, more word-driven posts talking about industry specific news and shorter posts about a new product or service. Any videos or images you can add will also help make your blog more three-dimensional. Just remember: Your blog should not be just about your business; you want to connect with your clients, not hard sell them your services. You can use complimentary blogging platforms such as Wordpress (**www.wordpress.com**) or Blogger (**www.blogger.com**) to create and maintain a blog.

In order for a blog to be an effective marketing tool, it is imperative for you to post at least two to three times a week. Blog posts should include keywords your potential clients and target markets use to find information on the services you provide.

You can also map out a year's worth of e-newsletter content, tweets, and public relations campaigns that are all built around the same editorial content topics to keep everything streamlined and in alignment.

## Article marketing

Use content you have created, and develop it into new articles; aim for at least one article per week. Popular topics for notaries include how-to articles and articles that cover specific steps or detailed information on topics relevant to your audience. For example, a notary may write an article on the top five ways to make sure that a document is legal.

You can use these articles to disseminate information via your e-newsletter, upload them to article directories, such as EzineArticles® (**www.ezinearticles.com**) and Amazines (**www.amazines.com**), use them on your blog, and post them on your social media networks. Make sure your articles are also rich with keywords. Article marketing is one of the most effective and least expensive ways to drive targeted traffic to your notary website. Your goal in using article marketing is to drive visitors to the appropriate page of your site — where your free offer sits. Your goal is to get them to request the free offer in exchange for gathering their information. You do this by including a strong call to action in the resource box of each article you submit online. This is also a lead-in for other marketing communication efforts and up-selling to your paid services.

You can also record the articles you write and repurpose them into videos and podcasts. Upload the podcasts to your blog and create an audio or video series that you can include on your blog, distribute in your e-newsletter, upload to YouTube, or send out as a special series of e-mail blasts to your subscriber list. Podcasts can also be uploaded and distributed on iTunes.

## Link building

On a weekly basis, visit business websites, blogs, and forums related to your business, niche, or industry. These are additional places where your audience is looking for information and another place where you can find information, as well as start building relationships with other notary companies. Post a relevant, valuable comment at least five sites per week. Forums and blog posts allow you to post your name, business name, and a link back to your website — again, driving traffic back to your website. This is an indirect way of promoting your business by positioning yourself as an expert and a resource while creating additional exposure for your business. You want your name, company name, and website address all over the sites that have anything to do with your business. If your potential clients are visiting these sites, you want them to see you there, too.

Sites of this nature also may offer an opportunity for you to become a guest author or article contributor, which allows you to use content you have to share your expertise with a new audience, gain the attention of your target market by positioning yourself as the expert you are, and broaden your reach.

## *Direct response*

You also need to focus on nurturing the your existing leads and the new ones you are gathering by consistently communicating with your database. You can communicate with your database by sending out autoresponders and promotional e-mails at least once or twice a month. Promotional e-mails may include a special offer on one of your notary services, announce the dates of an upcoming teleseminar, or incorporate a case study that illustrates a problem one of your clients faced and how your services resolved the problem. Promotions and case studies also can be included in the e-newsletter.

Building your website is just one step in creating a solid foundation for your business. The next chapter discusses how to grow your business from an operational standpoint.

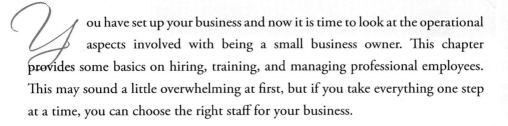

C H A P T E R   1 2 :

# Growing Your Notary Business

You have set up your business and now it is time to look at the operational aspects involved with being a small business owner. This chapter provides some basics on hiring, training, and managing professional employees. This may sound a little overwhelming at first, but if you take everything one step at a time, you can choose the right staff for your business.

## Successful Management Qualities

In a world where challenge and competition is common in a workplace, having a good management team is imperative. If management is such an important part of a business' success, what should a manager or management team have to make an organization successful?

Managers should understand being successful does not only mean assigning tasks or monitoring performances of employees. Rather, good managers should plan and motivate their employees with the same vision so everyone can aim for one main goal. It is unhealthy to dwell on limited problems. Good managers look at the big picture and ways to accomplish their long-term company goals. They live according to the mission of the organization and dedicate all their efforts to accomplishing that mission.

A good manager understands that to be effective, he or she must learn to attend to the team's needs. The manager realizes the organization is not a popularity contest and knows how to treat his or her employees with the utmost respect. He or she keeps his word and strives to recognize the employees' unique needs.

A manager will fail if he or she has poor communication skills. If a manager cannot talk to or connect with his or her employees, chances are the employees will not be able to connect with the manager. A good manager should learn how to communicate his or her job expectations and standards. From time to time, he or she should give feedback to his or her employees and should also seek and acknowledge feedback from his or her employees. In times of trouble around the workplace, communicating bad news in the most honest manner is exceedingly helpful. It is also ideal for managers to communicate using a language that exudes positive expectations.

Some managers do not understand that a business will fail if it is unable to develop team members. The success of the manager is also the success of the team. Some employees need coaching, motivation, discipline, assistance, or feedback. A good manager takes time to work and find a common ground among the staff members so that in the end, everybody wins. To become an effective manager, it is important to recognize the need to find that common ground with each team member.

Good managers are concerned with the professional advancement of their team members. This type of manager sees his or her employee not only for who they are, but who they can become. It is beneficial for the manager and the staff to have enough room for improvements, including changes of job performances, delegating special assignments, and developing action plans for promotions. A good manager possesses the ability to assess the strengths and weaknesses of his or her employees carefully and uses weaknesses to hone his or her staff for continuous improvements.

A good manager believes in the best assets and abilities of his or her employees. He or she is confident staff members are smart enough to take care of tasks. Employees should be given the chance to prove their worth. When problems arise, a good manager believes his or her staff can find possible solutions to those challenges. The more trust a manager puts in his or her employees, the better these employees will perform.

A good management team starts with a good manager. But a manager can never be a good manager without the cooperation of his team. The most important factor of a successful management team is the relationship of the manager and the team members.

It is vital for a manager to have a system in place that allows for an environment of free-flowing ideas. A good manager does not stifle his or her team's creativity. No matter how brilliant the manager is, he or she still does not know everything. A good manager realizes some of the best ideas come from the employees who are out there every day on the front lines of business.

It is important that ideas and contributions are rewarded. People need incentives. If you encourage an employee's idea or suggestion, give them ownership of the idea and being proactive; they will run with it and succeed.

# To Hire Employees or Not to Hire Employees: That Is the Question

When you open a business, you are taking a big step. Certain businesses — for instance a restaurant — need employees, and certain businesses, such as one-person computer repair business, do not need employees at all. There comes a time when your one-person business starts to grow, and you have to consider hiring employees. If you take on too much work and spread yourself too thin, you are making your business vulnerable to sloppiness and the possibility that your business could fail. Do not look at the situation with the mind-set that you are not capable of doing everything on your own. View this situation as a sign you are succeeding — your business is growing. Hiring employees could mean somebody helping you part time or someone you hire full time; your business load is what will dictate this.

One thing you need to consider is: How long do you need an employee? Your business might only need someone part time in the beginning. Analyze your work and your schedule. Determine what areas you need the most assistance with at this point. Is it just paperwork, organization, and general administrative assistance? Your starting point should be, "What are areas am I neglecting the most in my business?"

After your business is underway and you start going out to quote jobs or work in the field, you may decide that a phone answering machine is not enough. There are definite advantages in having someone in the office to answer the phones, call the vendors, do phone marketing, or set schedules for bidding. Some of this work cannot wait until dark when the outside jobs are done.

You may want to tiptoe into the role of employing an office worker. Part-time help is usually easy to come by. You may ask around among friends or relatives. Or, if you are reluctant to take a chance on a friend's recommendation, and you live in an urban or suburban area, place a classified ad in your local paper, online publication, or on a local/national site, such as Craigslist, at **www.craigslist.com**, or Monster, at **www.monster.com**. You will probably receive more job applications than you can handle.

Start the selection process before you place the ad by describing exactly what you want this employee to do, what experience he or she will need before starting, and what software programs or equipment skills the person will need to have. Also, remember that your office helper may well become the "face and voice" of your business. So, the person you choose should be able to get along with the public, in person, and especially on the phone. You may want someone who also can do cold calling to solicit business for an extra bonus if an appointment is actually set. Or, perhaps you would rather have a bookkeeper to take over some of the data-entry responsibilities. Whatever it is you want, write it down, read it over several times, and picture the kind of person you would feel comfortable with. Personality counts.

When you hire an employee, realize you might have to take the time to supervise them until you are sure they can work on their own. At first, a new employee could hinder your business flow because you will be stopping to work with and assist them. You should not be afraid to hire someone though. The most important thing is that you are comfortable with this change to your business.

## Hiring notaries with professional qualifications and attitudes

As a notary public, you are gaining a glimpse into people's lives; discretion will be of the utmost importance. Accordingly, only trained professionals should handle material as sensitive and private as legal document notarizing. Due to the delicate nature of some of the documents that are notarized — such as wills, affidavits, and divorce papers — it is important that only the most ethical people view and sign the documents. What this means for a company considering hiring additional notaries is that a vigorous screening process should be used to find the best notaries for the job.

When opening a notary business, there are certain qualifications that every notary has to have and, as previously discussed, regulations vary by state. When hiring new notaries for your business, it is necessary that each of them have the notary requirements for the state in which the business is operating. Hiring someone who is a certified notary public is only the first step.

It is a normal requirement for a notary to be bonded before becoming commissioned. Notaries working in a business where security can become an issue or where there could be the possibility of monetary loss are bonded. Therefore, for a notary, being bonded is insurance that guarantees competent job performance. The bond is guaranteeing that a certain amount of money will be paid if the notary does not perform his or her job properly. In other words, if the notary's client suffers a loss because of incompetent notarizations, the client will be able to collect for the client's attorney fees and any court settlements.

What protects the notary is errors and omissions insurance (E&O). If a notary's daily activities involve working with documents where there is the possibility of great financial loss (more than $25,000), a notary should consider E&O insurance. If all of these requirements are met, it is possible to know that only the best notaries are being used.

There are other considerations for hiring new notaries besides looking for the basic professional skills. The person's availability is a huge aspect to the job. Many customers will want notary services at times other than normal business hours. How willing the potential employee is to do the work at odd hours is an important factor to consider. Another factor to consider is the fact that some customers will not speak English. It is important to hire a few notaries fluent in languages that are common in your area of business. If all of these guidelines are followed, professionals will be hired and the unsuitable candidates will stay away.

Hiring professional employees is especially important in the notary business. Not only is it vital for the customers, but it is also vital for the legality of the business. A company can get into trouble for an employee's actions, even if the company was unaware of them. Therefore, it is exceedingly important to have a strict screening process when choosing notaries to hire.

Becoming a notary is not difficult, so it is imperative to weed out unsavory candidates. There are several ways to do this, including checking an applicant's notary licenses, looking at his or her experience and references, conducting background and drug testing, and performing rigorous interviews. The following four criteria can be used to choose the best people for the job.

## Licensing

The first thing to check when looking for competent employees is their licensing. Every person hired should have at least the minimum notary requirements for the state where the business is located. If the applicant has additional certification and licensing, this would mean they are more serious about the job and likely would be a better candidate for the company. Licensing is the most important requirement that all notaries in each business should have.

## Experience

The next thing to look at when hiring employees is their experience. Have they worked as a notary before? If so, for how long were they employed? Do they have any references from their previous employers saying they were good at their job? If a notary has good background experience, he or she will be likely to be a competent employee. Of course, the more experienced a notary is, the more payment he or she will expect. Consequently, if you do not have a large budget to work with, you may be forced to hire a novice notary public. However, it is more beneficial to have at least one experienced notary on staff.

## Criminal background check, credit history, and drug testing

To ensure you hire the best employees possible, use these common screening practices. A small company starting out might not have the money to pay a medical facility to do drug testing, but criminal record and credit checks cost less money than the drug testing and are effective at finding competent people. These tests can cost $9.95-$29.95 depending on the company you use for the background checks and are just another way to find the best people possible to help run the business.

# Interview

The last way to screen potential employees is through personal interviews. It is possible to tell a lot about someone from the way they present themselves in an interview. You can learn a lot about the potential employee by asking some basic questions, including "How does this type of work interest you?" or "How can you sum up your work history?" Of course, one important thing to bear in mind is that the most charismatic people are not always going to make the best employees. The charismatic people know how to make themselves look good, but they are not always the best workers. In an interview, it is possible to find out about a potential employee's past work experience, what they did, why they left, and much more information.

The interview process begins on the telephone, as you are setting a time for a personal meeting. The first thing to consider is the attitude of the person on the other end. Is he or she friendly or surly? Do not confuse an inability to articulate with a bad attitude. Someone may not have much formal education but have experience and a positive attitude that will overcome poor grammar. What is the overall demeanor of the person you are talking to on the telephone? Does this sound like a person you would like to be around? Some people may be shy about admitting they do not have much experience or some other negative. Lack of experience is not as big a drawback as someone whom you suspect is being evasive, for instance, trying to pass off work experience at a fast food restaurant as a qualification to work for you as an employee.

Why do they want the job? Do they have an interest in being a notary, or do they just need some money? Select the most suitable applicants before you schedule face-to-face meetings. You will want to know whether they have experience with the tools and equipment they will use as your employee.

During the personal interview, apply the same standards you would expect your customers to use. How is this person presenting himself or herself? Is the person clean? Is clothing torn or dirty? Does he or she look you in the eye? If the prospective employee claims to have experience, ask them two or three questions that require some knowledge to answer. You do not have to be challenging or harsh in your questioning. You can be friendly, even funny. You want to determine to the best of your ability whether this person is being honest with you. You might want to present a scenario and ask how the applicant would start, perform, and finish the task you describe.

Review the applicant's résumé and ask questions about gaps in work history or lack of recommendations or past employers. Someone who tries to turn that work history into a major qualification to work for you might not be as desirable as an employee. If you have the sense that your candidate is lying, be cautious about hiring him or her. It is easier to not hire someone in the first place than to fire him or her after the fact.

Following these guidelines will help a new company ensure they are hiring the best people possible for the job. Sometimes even people with good qualifications do not work out. This is not a reflection on your judgment skills or the company necessarily but just proof the person was not a good match for the job. Nonetheless, following these guidelines should help find the most competent notaries for a new business.

## Finding interns

Another route for companies to go is using interns who will usually work for either school credit or for pay. This type of position is beneficial for the intern because they learn the ins and outs of the notary business. This type of worker is beneficial since the company will be able to use his or her assistance for little or no expense because it is a part-time job. If you are looking for interns, it would be a good idea to check with your local college or university's career center and see if you would be able to post an advertisement for an internship position.

# What Is a Job Analysis?

Once you have hired employees and interns and they have worked for your company for a while, you will want to analyze their job performance. A job analysis means taking a job apart figuratively. Every aspect of the job is studied, and suggestions are made on how to improve it. It can also be used for training. Human resources would use a job analysis to study an employee's strengths and weaknesses and recommend changes where necessary. For example, in vocational rehabilitation, job analysis is used to determine if a person who has some limitations can do a particular job based on accommodations made. A good job analysis will be made after conducting interviews, written questionnaires, observation, and collecting information about any particular job.

After making a visual analysis and talking to the employee, the job analyst would make charts and graphs to help decide if the prospective employee is right for the job. The analyst would study the tasks a person conducts on the job and the skills and knowledge he or she has; his or her working conditions also are studied. It is important that it is legally appropriate to do what an analyst does.

Once you have analyzed everything and obtained the results, it is easy to convert the analysis into a job description, which will help you recruit potential employees. Any time you know exactly what a job requires, you can easily put that information on a job posting. You can advertise for the job, giving the description of what you need based upon the job analysis.

Not only will job analysis help you determine a job description for future hiring needs, but it also will help you determine how well a current employee is doing. If after the job analysis is complete and you determine an employee's work is satisfactory, you can consider offering that employee an incentive or bonus. However, if you discover one of your employees is not performing at the level you require, you will need to find a way to work with that employee to improve their productivity or even suspend or fire them. Because it is your business and your employees will answer to you, all work your employees perform reflects on you. If you are not happy with the work one of your employees has done and it is not up to the standards you hold yourself to, that employee should not be representing your company.

After you have hired employees and analyzed their performance, it is time to think of ways to reward employees for good work. One way to do that is by recognizing an employee as an "Employee of the Month."

# Internal Marketing for the Notary: That "Employee of the Month"

For businesses large and small, the efforts of employees represent the original vision and ambition of the founders. For the successful notary business, employees are considered the most important factor in the service the notary provides. Internal marketing offers employees the benefit of easy access and added value as the organization empowers employees to develop their personal goals while completing the business goals the company demands.

The fundamentals of internal marketing consist of enabling a workforce to increase their potential and increase current clients. Creating plans to satisfy both the client and the employee through self-sustaining service can result in a superior client interaction and end with the added satisfaction of the employee for the job well done. This effectively presents a company with an opportunity to get more for less with the correct implementation of a proven program of employee empowerment.

This type of employee empowerment policy has been proven to take a small business to the next level. When you realize the full benefits of internal marketing in a notary public business plan, your employees will be doing more than waiting for the next client. The empowered employee will seek out new and potential clients with an assertive, confident service. The clients you already have will be handled with a new enthusiasm because your notary employees will be able to see that their efforts are rewarded when they follow the empowerment policies implemented under the new internal marketing program.

The reputation of a notary public company rests with its employees and its performance. For the new notary business, empowerment from a proven internal marketing plan gives the employee the ability to build a positive client/vendor relationship from beginning to end. These interactions result in fewer client losses due to ineffective client interaction and unenthusiastic employees. A company can develop high-end clients while giving back to the employees who have the most interaction with those same high-end clients.

The best way to increase your company morale is to research and develop a program of employee empowerment in your notary public business. Give rewards to employees who are going above and beyond their duties. Offer your workforce incentives for discovering new clients. Work from within your small group and find out how each member can reach a segment of people you need as clients. After you find new ways to involve your employees in ways to improve business, plan a worker day celebration, or begin to find ways to promote or reward your workforce individually. These are the ways smart businesses get the most from investing in people. Develop a team of individuals who all work toward the benefit of the whole because they feel they will ultimately benefit from their efforts.

The notary with excellent business and marketing acumen can see the benefits of a successful internal marketing program in all aspects of the business. When your workforce is working to be successful as they make your company successful, your company will be well represented by all employees. Your new team will work together to find new clients, handle clients more effectively, and in general, be a happier group of people. Your business will benefit from the added pride your employees have in the work. Your clients will return more frequently because of the service they received. New clients will find ways to see your information because the successful internal marketing involves new sales ideas and programs, too. For the notary public, internal marketing improves integrity and the perception new clients have of your business from the moment it is implemented. Without it, you may find yourself with only your employees to talk to.

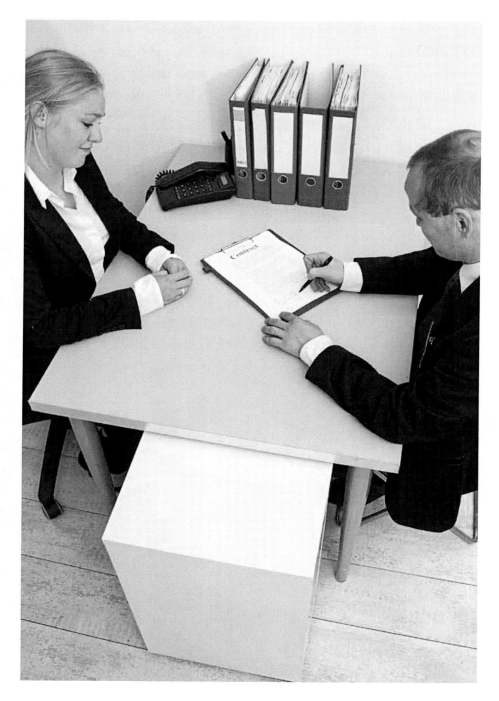

# Conclusion

## The Future of the Notary Public

The Internet age and the drive to reduce paperwork have brought a new role for future notaries. The modern day notaries are finding themselves responsible for identifying digital signatures in addition to original signature. The National Notary Association (NNA) is developing the Enjoa Digital E-Notarization journal platform and implementing ENS electronic notary commission information for all notaries who perform electronic notarial acts in order to accommodate what is expected to become more common in the future. Though e-notarization is in its infancy, its future looks promising. With more and more transactions occurring on the Internet, there is a growing need for notarization on a global scale.

As long as there are transactions, the need to securitize these transactions exists. The notary public serves the important purpose of being an independent witness and fulfills a vital role of securing the transaction by authenticating the record of the transaction. Authentication of the signer of a document by a notary public does not make it legal, but it does make it secure. This is why that since the time of Egyptian civilization, notaries have played a major role in preventing transaction frauds.

The NNA constantly works to improve laws and rules of notarization to make it an important part of document security. The organization works with criminal agencies, the FBI, and other security agencies to improve methods of securing documents through notarization.

# Roles Notaries Play in National Security by Detecting ID Fraud

Identity fraud is one of the most popular ways for people to commit crimes. It is rather easy to steal someone's identity. Notaries play a big role in preventing ID fraud because for every document they notarize, they must ensure the correct parties are signing for it. This is how they help prevent fraud using legal documents.

One of the responsibilities of a notary public is to ensure that people who come in to sign documents are the right parties. If the notary suspects that there is any suspicious identity business going on, he or she is responsible for refusing to sign the documents. If he or she signed just anything presented to him or her, it would be possible to sign over properties and other important things to people who should not be involved in such a transaction. It is important for a notary to check the IDs of each person who comes in to get something signed and notarized. If a notary notarizes something for the wrong party, he or she is held responsible and can and lose his or her license and certification. So not only is there an incentive to check the identities of everyone who comes in so that the right people get the right papers, but it also keeps the notary in business. Even if you did not lose your license, if your clients learn that you signed a document for the wrong person, then he or she will lose confidence in you and go to another notary. That is why it is very important to check the identities of all people signing documents, as well as the validity of the documents.

The other main responsibility of a notary public is to check the documents being notarized. Even if the identities of the parties who want the notarization are matched to the documents, it is still important to see if the documents they bring in are eligible to be notarized. You would not want to notarize the deed of a house for someone only to find out that the deed belonged to someone else. Another important task for the notary public is to check the documents for authenticity. Some notaries work with a legal consultant to ensure the right people are using the proper documents. This tag-team method is probably the best way to avoid identity fraud of any kind.

These identity theft prevention methods are the main ways a notary public can ensure the proper people are notarizing the appropriate documents. It is easy to watch for the signs of someone who is trying to get something notarized that should not be. If the people seem to be overly nervous, or if they try to rush you, then you might want to take some extra time to go over exactly what it is they want notarized. If these methods are followed, then identify theft and ID fraud through notarizations will be cut down and eliminated.

If you follow these practices as a notary public, then you will be doing your part to help prevent ID fraud.

# Notaries in the Electronic Age

Because of communication via the Internet, will people stop traveling? Because of the ease of the Internet, will the need for the United States Postal Service become obsolete? Will the need for a notary public completely disappear in the electronic age? The answer to these questions is no. The electronic age has changed our everyday lives, and with those changes, it has brought new challenges to authentication requirements. The new methods still require the service of the notary public. The emerging method in our global society is digital time stamping. If the document is to be converted to a different format, for example, hard copy, permission should be sought from the author of the document with the earliest time stamp.

With the dangers of digital piracy and tampering looming in the horizon, time stamping for electronic documents will soon become a major service provided by notary publics in the future.

# Making a Sound Career Choice

When you were growing up and someone asked you what you wanted to be when you grew up, no one ever said a notary public. Nevertheless, there is a time and point in one's life where you have to do a self-assessment to discover and determine what path your life will follow. Perhaps a family member, a friend, or a significant other has suggested career opportunities that would be perfect for you. Everyone always has an answer.

These days, it is normal for people to have multiple careers over the course of life. Most of these careers are completely different from each other. Anything that you love to do and that earns an income is a good career choice. No one wants to wake up every day and dread going to work. Not everyone thinks of being a notary as a career per se, and not everyone is cut out to be a notary. But if you are interested in law and feel good about being in constant touch with people in all walks of life, this is an excellent career choice. Many advantages come with being a notary public agent.

A notary public agency is an excellent choice for those who are outgoing by nature and have good people skills. There are few career choices other than those in hospitality or the food service industry that offer you a more conducive environment to interact with people. Unlike sales people, here your clients pursue you, not the other way around, which makes the career enjoyable and profitable.

# Conclusion

The requirements to be a notary are not rigorous. This is yet another positive factor when you make this your career choice. It is true that you need to be aware of how documents are notarized and that there is the minimum requirement that you understand law and its fundamentals. However, you do not need to be a lawyer to work as a notary public.

The bottom line is that the income from this business can be wonderful. If you work an average of about 10 hours a week, you could easily earn $50,000 per year. This is when you charge only $150.00 per appointment. The fees can be more as you establish your business and expand your working hours. This means the world is your oyster. Honestly, this career, as any other career, is what you make of it.

Too many of us are unhappy with our jobs and are paid a pittance of what we truly deserve. By choosing a career as a notary, you will be a distinguished member of society and earn a fair and decent wage for the service you are providing to people. Essentially, this book is dedicated to the proposition that you will be a paid a fair dollar for an honest day of work.

# APPENDIX A :
# Glossary

**acknowledge:** When a notary verifies that the signer is who he or she claims to be

**acknowledgment:** The portion of the document that the notary signs

**acknowledgment certificate:** A certificate signed by an authorized official; it states in form stipulated by law that an official obtained the acknowledgment of the person(s) who signed the agreement.

**adjustable rate mortgage (ARM):** A mortgage rate where the interest can fluctuate, depending on the prime rate

**administer:** To give or apply in a formal way

**affiant:** The person signing the affidavit, swearing to its truth

**affidavit:** A document where the signer swears under oath to its truth

**affirmation:** A declaration that replaces a sworn statement by a person objecting to taking an oath

**affix:** To secure to another; to append

**amortization:** A repayment plan where the interest and a portion of the principal are included in each periodic payment using a mathematical formula

**annual percentage rate (APR):** What the cost of credit is based on a yearly rate. A lower APR is normally better.

**apostille:** A certificate that proves the authenticity of a notary's signature and seal

**appointment:** The act of appointing for an office or position

**appraisal:** A statement made by a professional appraiser stating his/her opinion of the property's value

**attest:** To recognize to be correct, true, or genuine; confirm.

**attorney-in-fact:** The power of attorney (POA) (or letter of attorney in common law structures or mandate in civil law systems) is an agreement to act on someone else's behalf in a legal or business matter.

**authenticate:** To attest or validate as authentic

**balloon mortgage:** A type of mortgage with equal monthly payments and a lump sum due at the maturity date of the loan

**beneficiary:** The person or entity that receives the assets and/or profit when there is a distribution

**caveat:** A warning or caution

**certificate, notarial:** Appears at the end of a notarized document stating the specifics of the notarization and is signed and sealed by the notary

**certified copy:** A deed, certificate, record, or document certified by a notary to be a factual and accurate copy of the original

**certificate of title:** Commonly used to indicate ownership of a vehicle, a document that specifies the vehicle's type, engine number, and the name and address of the registered owner and lien holder

**civil action:** A lawsuit for the purpose of security of private rights and recompense for their violation

**civil liability:** The accountability and requirement to make compensation to another person for damages caused by offensive acts

**clear title:** Indicates ownership of real property and that no other persons can claim ownership

**closing:** The final step in the purchase of real estate. It includes the completion of all documentation and exchange of any remaining funds.

**closing agent:** A person or company responsible for the management of a range of activities required for completing the sale of a house or other type of real estate property

**CNSA or certified notary signing agent:** A person who has been certified by a company that trains notaries

**commercial paper:** A negotiable unsecured promissory note with short maturity

**commission:** A document describing the notary's appointment and term of office

**conveyance:** A broad term for any written document transferring property from one party to another

**credible (identifying) witness:** A person whose testimony is likely to be authentic based on subjective factors such as experience, knowledge, training, and demeanor

**deed:** A document that transfers ownership to another person. There are two kinds of deeds: a warranty deed, guaranteeing the grantor owns title; and quitclaim deed, transferring only the real property interest that the grantor actually has.

**defendant:** The party who is being sued (in civil court) or charged with a crime (criminal court)

**dispose:** To record and store in an orderly manner; in relation to a notarial journal, to keep on record for seven years

**down payment:** The portion of the price of the real estate that is paid with cash up front and does not finance

**duress:** Constraint by threat, coercion

**easement:** A right that gives a person other than the owner access to and over a property

**embosser:** A pliers-like device squeezed together with paper between the jaws, makes raised areas and indentations on paper; used as a protection device; not an official notary seal, but may be used in addition to the official notary seal

**encumbrance:** Something that affects or restricts the title to a property (example: mortgage, lease or easement)

**errors and omission insurance:** A form of liability insurance that protects you as a notary from any errors or mistakes you might make

**escrow:** The money deposited with a third party that gets delivered upon fulfillment of prearranged terms

**fair market value:** The price at which a buyer and seller are willing to do business

**felony:** A serious crime, such as murder, illegal weapons possession, or arson

**finance charge:** The amount that the loan costs the borrower

**fixed-rate mortgage:** A mortgage where the interest rate remains the same throughout the duration of the loan

**foreclosure:** A legal act that occurs when the borrower is in default of a mortgage and loses his or her interest in the property

**grantee:** The person to whom property interest is conveyed

**grantor:** The person who conveys the interest in property

**interest rate:** The percentage that is charged periodically for a credit or loan

**journal of notarial acts:** Notarial journal arranged by law to document notarial acts

**jurat:** A notarial act where the notary certifies having viewed the signing of a document and administered an oath/affirmation where the signer declares the document is truthful

**jurisdiction:** The area where a notary is authorized and licensed to work

**lien:** The justified right to acquire another's property if a debt or contract is not discharged

**loose certificate:** When no notary wording and/or an incorrect notary wording is present on a document, the notary can attach a separate sheet of paper with the notary certificate amended to it.

**locus sigilli (L.S.):** Latin term meaning "place of the seal." In many states, instead of sealing deeds, writs, and other papers or documents requiring it, a scroll is made in which the letters L.S. are printed or written, which is an abbreviation of *locus sigilli*. This indicates where the official notary seal imprint is to be placed.

**misconduct:** Behavior that is not in accordance with accepted moral or professional standards

**misdemeanor:** An offense of lesser gravity than a felony

**mortgagee:** The person who receives the mortgage (a.k.a. "the borrower")

**mortgagor:** The institution that gives the mortgage (a.k.a. "the lender")

**note (promissory):** A written agreement consisting of a promise on the signer's part to pay the named person or institution a specified amount of money on a given date, or on demand of lender

**notary journal:** An official record book of notarizations performed by a notary

**notary public:** A person legally empowered to witness signatures and certify a document's validity and to take depositions

**notary seal:** An official stamp or embosser official stamp used by a notary to seal notarizations

**notary signing agent:** An agent whose purpose is to acquire a formal signature of an appearer to a document

**oath:** A sworn promise of the truthfulness of a given statement made in the presence of a notary

**official notary seal:** An official stamp or embosser used by a notary to seal notarizations. It must be kept under the direct and exclusive control of the notary.

**origination fee:** A fee paid by the borrower to the lender for the processing fees regarding the loan application

**personal appearance:** The signer of the document to be notarized must appear in person and in front of the notary.

**personal knowledge:** When a notary is familiar with the signer enough so that there is no doubt regarding the person's identity

**personally known:** Knowledge of an individual resulting from communications with that individual adequate to eradicate every reasonable doubt that the individual has the identity claimed

**plaintiff:** The party who is suing (in civil court) or charging another party with a crime (criminal court)

**points:** The one-time fee charged by the lender to increase the yield of the loan. Commonly, one point is the equivalent to 1 percent of the mortgage.

**positive identification:** Knowing the signer of a document without any doubt of their identity

**power of attorney:** A legal document that gives the right to a person to act on the behalf of another

**principal:** The amount remaining on a loan, less the interest

**public record:** Any documents that are made available for the public to view

**reconveyance:** Returning the title to the trustor when the note issued by a deed of trust is satisfied

**recording:** When a deed, mortgage, or other legal document is noted in the registrar's office, making the document public record

**refinancing:** When one loan is paid off by taking on a second loan with a lower interest rate, it uses the original property as security.

**representative capacity:** The ability to act on behalf of another person or legal entity as in the case of a corporation, trust, or partnership

**resignation:** A written formal notice of one's intention to resign

**reverse mortgage:** A loan intended for older individuals with a large amount of equity in their home. Repayment does not go into effect until the property is sold or the individual relocates to a retirement community.

**revoke:** To cancel or rescind

**right to cancel/right of rescission:** An option that gives the borrower three business days to cancel the loan

**sanctions:** Monetary fines, levied against a party to a legal action or their attorney, for violating rules of procedure, or for abusing the judicial process

**satisfactory evidence:** The proof needed to satisfy credibility beyond a reasonable doubt

**second mortgage:** Mortgage that is subsidiary to a first mortgage

**security:** Property that is used as collateral for a loan

**signature by mark:** An "X" or other mark made by signer who is unable to sign his or her name; must be witnessed by a notary and at least one other witness

**signing agent:** An agent whose function is to obtain a formal signature of an appearer to a document

**signing service:** A company that subcontracts signing appointments to "loan document signers" (notary public) for signing of loan documents and notarization

**S.S. or SCT:** Latin term *Silicet* means "in particular" or "namely"; where a notarization is performed (e.g., "jurisdiction")

**subscribe:** To sign one's name in attestation, testimony, or consent

**subscribing witness:** A person who witnesses the signing of a document and is willing to testify to that fact; a person who appears before the notary on behalf of the principal

**suspend:** To stop something or make something ineffective, usually for a short time

**swear/sworn:** To take an oath

**testimonium clause:** The concluding clause of an instrument beginning with the words: "In witness where-of...."

**title:** Written document that proves ownership of property

**title search:** A process of investigation that includes the history of ownership of a specific piece of property. A title search includes looking for any liens, unpaid claims, problems, or restrictions that can interfere with the seller's ability to transfer the property free and clear to a new buyer.

**trustee:** The holder who controls property for the benefit of someone else

**unauthorized or unlawful practice of law (UPL):** A person who is not a legal professional who dispenses legal advice or prepares a legal document

**underwriting:** The evaluation of a loan at the time of application to determine the amount of risk the lender stands to incur; normally involves a credit check on the borrower(s) and the quality of the intended property

**venue:** The geographic location (state and county) where both the notary and the signer are located when the notarial act occurs

**verification:** The evidence that proves something is true or correct

**waiver of fees:** A statement that gives up the right to pay fees for notarial services

**witness:** A person who observes an act as it occurs

# APPENDIX B:
# State-by-State
# Notary Specifics

*A*ppendix B contains listings for all of the individual state's websites where you can get up-to-date information on your state's requirements. You should consult the website for any changes in the notary application process and any updates regarding notary laws and provisions. Also, note that any recommended fees not stated can be set reasonably by the individual notary, though the fees must remain consistent.

## Alabama

| Eligibility requirements: | 18 years of age |
| | One-day minimum residency |
| | Must be endorsed by three county residents |
| | Application process: must be appointed and commissioned by the probate judge of your county. Visit site for specific county's application materials and process: **www.sos.state.al.us/vb/officials/index.aspx.** |
| Notary provisions: | Length of commission is four years. |
| | Seal requirements: embosser |

| | |
|---|---|
| | Journal requirements: required by law |
| | $10,000 bond required |
| **Notary fee guidelines:** | Acknowledgments: $.50 |
| | Jurats: $.50 |
| | Oaths and affirmations: $.50 |
| | Protests: $1.50 + postage |

# Alaska

| | |
|---|---|
| **Eligibility requirements:** | 18 years of age |
| | 30-day minimum residency |
| | Must be legal resident of the United States and Alaska resident |
| **Application process:** | Meet eligibility requirements. |
| | Obtain notary bond. |
| | Complete application form. |
| | Submit both with the application fee. |
| | For detailed information, visit **http://ltgov.alaska.gov/treadwell/notaries.** |
| **Notary provisions:** | Length of commission is four years. |
| | Seal requirements: embosser or inked stamp |
| | Journal requirements: required by law |
| | $1,000 bond required |
| **Notary fee guidelines:** | No fee schedule provided. According to Alaska's state website regarding notary fees: |
| | "Alaska Statutes do not address this subject for notaries without limitation except that a published fee schedule must be provided to the signer prior to the performance of the notarization if a notary intends to collect a fee for their services (AS 44.50.062 (4)). Statute does state that Limited Governmental Notaries may not charge for notarization." |

# Arizona

| Eligibility requirements: | 18 years of age |
| --- | --- |
| | No minimum residency |
| | No felony conviction |
| Application process: | Meet eligibility requirements. |
| | Read Arizona Notary Handbook (available for online download). |
| | Complete application. |
| | Obtain notary bond. |
| | Send completed application, fee, and original bond certification to the secretary of state's office. |
| | For detailed information, visit **www.azsos.gov/business_services/Notary.** |
| Notary provisions: | Length of commission is four years. |
| | Seal requirements: inked stamp |
| | Journal requirements: required by law |
| | $5,000 bond required |
| Notary fee guidelines: | Acknowledgments: $2 |
| | Jurats: $2 |
| | Oaths and affirmations: $2 |

# Arkansas

| Eligibility requirements: | 18 years of age |
| --- | --- |
| | No minimum residency |
| | Must be U.S. citizen |
| Application process: | Meet eligibility requirements |
| | Read Arkansas Notary Handbook (available for online download). |
| | Complete application form. |

|  | Obtain surety bond. |
|---|---|
|  | Send completed application, fee, and proof of bond to secretary of state. |
|  | For detailed information, visit **www.sosweb.state.ar.us/corp_ucc_notary.html**. |
| **Notary provisions:** | Length of commission is ten years. |
|  | Seal requirements: embossed or ink stamp |
|  | Journal requirements: recommended |
|  | $7,500 bond required |
| **Notary fee guidelines:** | Acknowledgments: $5 |
|  | Jurats: $5 |
|  | Oaths and affirmations: $5 |
|  | Protests: $5 + $5 notice of protest |

# California

| **Eligibility requirements:** | 18 years of age |
|---|---|
|  | No minimum residency |
|  | Must past state-issued exam for each term of your commission |
|  | Must provide fingerprints for background check |
| **Application process:** | Meet eligibility requirements. |
|  | Complete training course (mandatory). |
|  | Pass a state-issued notary exam. |
|  | Complete application form. |
|  | Submit application form along with fee, two-inch by two-inch passport-style photo of yourself, and fingerprints for background check. |
|  | File notary oath and bond with secretary of state. |
|  | For detailed information, visit **www.sos.ca.gov/business/notary/notary.htm**. |

| Notary provisions: | Length of commission is four years. |
| --- | --- |
| | Seal requirements: embosser or ink stamp (ink stamp is preferred for reproducibility on a photocopy) |
| | Journal requirements: required by law |
| | $15,000 bond required |
| Notary fee guidelines: | Acknowledgments: $10 |
| | Jurats: $10 |
| | Oaths and affirmations: $10 |
| | Protests: $10 + $5 for notice of nonpayment + $5 for recording |

# Colorado

| Eligibility requirements: | 18 years of age |
| --- | --- |
| | State residency required |
| | Must be able to read and write in English |
| | No lifetime felony convictions |
| | No misdemeanors in the past five years |
| | Never had a prior notary commission revoked |
| Application process: | Meet eligibility requirements. |
| | Familiarize yourself with the state's notary laws. |
| | Complete application form. |
| | Submit application form, filing fee, and photo identification to the secretary of state's office. |
| | For detailed information, visit **http://www.sos.state.co.us/pubs/notary/notaryHome.html**. |
| Notary provisions: | Length of commission is four years. |
| | Seal requirements: embosser or ink stamp |
| | Journal requirements: required only for acknowledgments on documents regarding titles on real property |
| | No bond requirement |

| Notary fee guidelines: | Acknowledgments: $5 |
|---|---|
| | Jurats: $5 |
| | Oaths and affirmations: $5 |

# Connecticut

| Eligibility requirements: | 18 years of age |
|---|---|
| | No minimum residency |
| | Must score 100 percent on notary exam |
| | Must be endorsed by a public official or reputable person |
| **Application process:** | Meet eligibility requirements. |
| | Complete application form. |
| | Pay the application fee. |
| | Successfully pass the state-administered exam. |
| | For detailed information, visit **www.sots.ct.gov/sots/cwp/view.asp?a=3184&q=392266**. |
| **Notary provisions:** | Length of commission is five years. |
| | Seal requirements: embosser or ink stamp |
| | Journal requirements: recommended by state |
| | No bond requirement |
| **Notary fee guidelines:** | Acknowledgments: $5 |
| | Jurats: $5 |
| | Oaths and affirmations: $5 |
| | Protests: $5 |

# Delaware

| | |
|---|---|
| **Eligibility requirements:** | 18 years of age |
| | No minimum residency, but non-resident must work in the state |
| | Endorsed with two letters of recommendation |
| **Application process:** | Meet eligibility requirements. |
| | Complete application form. |
| | Obtain two letters of reference in individual sealed envelopes |
| | Forward the application, fee, and your letters of reference to the secretary of state's office. |
| | For detailed information, visit **http://notary.delaware.gov/default.shtml**. |
| **Notary provisions:** | Length of commission is two years for your first term, two or four years each subsequent term. |
| | Seal requirements: embosser or ink stamp |
| | Journal requirements: recommended |
| | No bond requirement |
| **Notary fee guidelines:** | Acknowledgments: $5 |
| | Jurats: $5 |
| | Oaths and affirmations; $5 |
| | Protests: $5 |

# Florida

| | |
|---|---|
| **Eligibility requirements:** | 18 years of age |
| | No minimum residency |
| | No exam, though first-time applicants must take a three-hour course (online or in classroom) |
| | Must be endorsed by one character witness |
| | A noncitizen applicant must supply declaration of domicile. |

| Application process: | Meet eligibility requirements. |
| --- | --- |
| | Fill out notary application and bond forms. |
| | Successfully complete the required course. |
| | Submit application form, bond forms, certification of course completion, and fee to the National Notary Association (NNA). |
| | For detailed information, visit **http://notaries.dos.state.fl.us.** |
| Notary provisions: | Length of commission is four years. |
| | Seal requirements: inked stamp |
| | Journal requirements: recommended by state |
| | $7,500 bond requirement |
| Notary fee guidelines: | Acknowledgments: $10 |
| | Jurats: $10 |
| | Oaths and affirmations: $10 |

**Notaries in Florida may perform marriage ceremonies within the state boundaries. **

# Georgia

| Eligibility requirements: | 18 years of age |
| --- | --- |
| | No minimum residency |
| | Must be endorsed by two adult county citizens |
| Application process: | Meet eligibility requirements . |
| | Complete application form. |
| | Submit application form (no bond is needed in Georgia) to clerk of superior court in their county of residence. |
| | For detailed information, visit **www.gsccca.org/Projects/aboutnp.asp**. |
| Notary provisions: | Length of commission is four years. |
| | Seal requirements: embosser or ink stamp |
| | Journal requirements: recommended by state |

| | |
|---|---|
| | No bond requirement |
| **Notary fee guidelines:** | Acknowledgments: $2 |
| | Jurats: $2 |
| | Oaths and affirmations: $2 |

# Hawaii

| | |
|---|---|
| **Eligibility requirements:** | 18 years of age |
| | No minimum residency requirement, but must be a resident of Hawaii |
| | Must pass state exam |
| | Need to be endorsed with a letter of recommendation |
| **Application process:** | Meet eligibility requirements. |
| | Complete application form. |
| | Submit application materials. |
| | Once your application is approved, you must take and successfully pass the notary exam with a score of at least 80 percent. |
| | For detailed information, visit **http://hawaii.gov/ag/notary.** |
| **Notary provisions:** | Length of commission is four years. |
| | Seal requirements: embosser or inked stamp |
| | Journal requirements: required by law |
| | $1,000 bond requirement |
| **Notary fee guidelines:** | Acknowledgments: $5 |
| | Jurats: $5 |
| | Oaths and affirmations: $5 |
| | Protests: $5 + $5 for each notice and certified copy of protest |

# Idaho

| Eligibility requirements: | 18 years of age |
| --- | --- |
| | No minimum residency |
| | Must be a U.S. citizen |
| | Must be able to read and write English |
| Application process: | Meet eligibility requirements. |
| | Complete the application form. |
| | Purchase a rubber stamp seal. |
| | Obtain $10,000 notary bond. |
| | Submit completed application, application fee, and signed bond to secretary of state for processing. |
| | For detailed information, visit **www.sos.idaho.gov/notary/npindex.htm**. |
| Notary provisions: | Length of commission is six years. |
| | Seal requirements: inked stamp |
| | Journal requirements: recommended by the state |
| | $10,000 bond required |
| Notary fee guidelines: | Acknowledgments: $2 |
| | Jurats: $2 |
| | Oaths and affirmations: $2 |

# Illinois

| Eligibility requirements: | 18 years of age |
| --- | --- |
| | 30-day minimum residency |
| | Must be able to read and write in English |
| | No felony convictions |
| Application process: | Meet eligibility requirements. |
| | Complete application form. |
| | Obtain a notary bond in the amount of $5,000. |

| | |
|---|---|
| | Submit application materials to the secretary of state, where the application will be approved and filed with the county clerk in which the applicant resides. |
| | For detailed information, visit **www.cyberdriveillinois.com/departments/index/notary/home.html**. |
| **Notary provisions:** | Length of commission is four years (one year for out-of-state residents). |
| | Seal requirements: inked stamp |
| | Journal requirements: recommended by state |
| | $5,000 bond requirement |
| **Notary fee guidelines:** | Acknowledgments: $1 |
| | Jurats: $1 |
| | Oaths and affirmations: $1 |

# Indiana

| | |
|---|---|
| **Eligibility requirements:** | 18 years of age |
| | Must be a legal resident |
| | Cannot hold another public office |
| **Application process:** | Meet eligibility requirements. |
| | Complete application form. |
| | Obtain notary bond. |
| | Submit application form, application fee, and proof of bond to secretary of state's office. |
| | For detailed information, visit **www.in.gov/sos/business/2378.htm**. |
| **Notary provisions:** | Length of commission is eight years. |
| | Seal requirements: embosser or inked stamp |
| | Journal requirements: recommended by state |
| | $5,000 bond requirement |

| Notary fee guidelines: | Acknowledgments: $2 |
| --- | --- |
| | Jurats: $2 |
| | Oaths and affirmations: $2 |

# Iowa

| Eligibility requirements: | 18 years of age |
| --- | --- |
| | No minimum residency |
| Application process: | Meet eligibility requirements. |
| | Complete application form. |
| | Submit application form along with application fee to secretary of state's office. |
| | For detailed information, visit **www.sos.state.ia.us/notaries/notary_forms.html**. |
| Notary provisions: | Length of commission is three years (one year for qualified nonresident). |
| | Seal requirements: embosser or ink stamp |
| | Journal requirements: recommended by state |
| | No bond required |
| Notary fee guidelines: | No fee schedule provided, though according to Iowa's website regarding notary fees: |
| | "A notary in Iowa may charge a reasonable fee for their services. However, a notary cannot refuse to perform a service because a person is not a client/customer nor may the notary's employer restrict the notary from providing services because a person is not a client/customer of the employer." |

# Kansas

| Eligibility requirements: | 18 years of age |
|---|---|
| | No minimum residency |
| | Must be able to read and write in English |
| | No felony convictions |
| | No previous loss of professional license |
| Application process: | Meet eligibility requirements. |
| | Obtain notary bond in the amount of $7,500. |
| | Obtain a notary stamp. |
| | Complete notary application. |
| | Submit application form, filing fee, and proof of bond to secretary of state's office. |
| | For detailed information, visit **www.kssos.org/business/business_notary.html**. |
| Notary provisions: | Length of commission is four years. |
| | Seal requirements: embosser or ink stamp |
| | Journal requirements: recommended by the state |
| | $7,500 bond requirement |
| Notary fee guidelines: | No fee provided. There is no statutory fee in the state of Kansas according to their website. There is no prohibition against a notary public charging a fee. Consequently, a notary public may charge a reasonable fee. |

# Kentucky

| Eligibility requirements: | 18 years of age |
|---|---|
| | No minimum residency |
| | Must be endorsed by circuit judge, legislator, or county official |
| Application process: | Meet eligibility requirements. |
| | Complete application form. |

| | |
|---|---|
| | Submit application form and filing fee to office of the secretary of state. |
| | For detailed information, visit **http://sos.ky.gov/adminservices/notaries**. |
| **Notary provisions:** | Length of commission is four years. |
| | Seal requirements: optional |
| | Journal requirements: recommended by state |
| | Bond requirement varies by county |
| **Notary fee guidelines:** | Acknowledgments: $.50 |
| | Jurats: $.50 |
| | Oaths and affirmations: $.50 |
| | Protests: $.50 + $.75 for recording and $.25 per notice of protest |

# Louisiana

| | |
|---|---|
| **Eligibility requirements:** | 18 years of age |
| | No minimum residency |
| | Must be endorsed by district judge |
| | Must pass exam if not an attorney |
| **Application process:** | Meet eligibility requirements. |
| | Obtain and complete application. |
| | Take notary exam. |
| | Obtain your notary bond. |
| | Execute two oath of office forms. |
| | File one oath of office and notary bond with your parish clerk of court. |
| | File the second oath of office form, along with certificate of competency from district court judge, official signature page, original or certified copy of your bond signed by the parish clerk of court, or an error and omissions policy and filing fee to the secretary of state. |

| | |
|---|---|
| | For detailed information, visit **www.sos.louisiana.gov/tabid/70/Default.aspx**. |
| **Notary provisions:** | Length of commission is for life. |
| | Seal requirements: recommended |
| | Journal requirements: required by law in Orleans Parish until December 31, 2008, recommended elsewhere |
| | $10,000 bond requirement |
| **Notary fee guidelines:** | No fee schedule provided, yet reasonable fees may be applied. |

**Notaries in the West Feliciana Parish may perform wedding ceremonies within parish borders. **

# Maine

| | |
|---|---|
| **Eligibility requirements:** | 18 years of age |
| | No minimum residency |
| | Must pass exam |
| | Must be endorsed by registered voter, elected official, municipal clerk, and registrar of voters |
| | Municipal clerk or registrar of voters must affix seal of municipality as proof of residency |
| **Application process:** | Meet eligibility requirements. |
| | Complete application form. |
| | Submit application form along with application fee to the secretary of state. |
| | If approved, applicant will receive his or her commission paperwork via postal mail. |
| | For detailed information, visit **www.maine.gov/sos/cec/notary/notaries.html**. |

| Notary provisions: | Length of commission is seven years. |
| --- | --- |
| | Seal requirements: recommended |
| | Journal requirements: required to keep journal for all marriages performed; other acts are recommended |
| | No bond required |
| Notary fee guidelines: | Protests: $1.50 |
| | No other fee schedule indicated, but according to Maine's Notary Handbook, the following is stated in regard to fees: |
| | There is no schedule of fees that a notary public must charge. The fee of a $1.50 for lawsuits will provide notification of parties, creation of certificate, and the recording proceedings. |
| | It is up to each individual notary public to set his or her own fees. Therefore, it is appropriate to charge fees that are fair and flexible. |
| | Due to the fact that notaries in the state of Maine can set their own pricing structures, persons seeking their services should have some assurance on the fees. |

**Notaries in the state of Maine may perform marriage ceremonies within the state boundaries.**

# Maryland

| Eligibility requirements: | 18 years of age |
| --- | --- |
| | No minimum residency |
| | Must be endorsed by a local state senator |
| Application process: | Meet eligibility requirements |
| | Complete application form. |
| | Submit application form along with processing fee to the senator of the applicant's senatorial district. |
| | After application is approved, applicant must take oath prior to being able to work as a notary. |

| | For detailed information, visit **www.sos.state.md.us/Notary/Notary.aspx**. |
|---|---|
| **Notary provisions:** | Length of commission is four years. |
| | Seal requirements: embosser or ink stamp |
| | Journal requirements: required by law |
| | No bond requirement |
| **Notary fee guidelines:** | Acknowledgments: $2 |
| | Jurats: $2 |
| | Oaths and affirmations: $2 |

# Massachusetts

| | |
|---|---|
| **Eligibility requirements:** | 18 years of age |
| | No minimum residency |
| | Must be endorsed by a lawyer and three others |
| **Application process:** | Meet eligibility requirements. |
| | Complete application form. |
| | Submit application form, along with references and resume to Notary Public Office. |
| | If application is approved, applicant will receive information via postal mail regarding instructions for being sworn in and how to pay commission fee. |
| | For detailed information, visit **www.sec.state.ma.us/pre/prenot/notidx.htm**. |
| **Notary provisions:** | Length of commission is seven years. |
| | Seal requirements: rubber stamp and/or embosser |
| | Journal requirements: required |
| | No bond requirement |

| Notary fee guidelines: | Protests: $2 maximum for protest of $500 or more, $1.50 maximum for protest under $500 |
| | No other fee schedule provided, though reasonable fees may be applied |

# Michigan

| Eligibility requirements: | 18 years of age |
| | No minimum residency |
| | Must be able to read and write in English |
| | Have no misdemeanor or felony convictions |
| Application process: | Meet eligibility requirements. |
| | Complete application form. |
| | Obtain a bond in the amount of $10,000, and file it with your respective county clerk. |
| | The county clerk will administer an oath to you and then fill out the appropriate portion of your application. |
| | Once all of your paperwork is complete, send application with processing fee to department of state's office. |
| | For detailed information, visit www.michigan.gov/sos/0,1607,7-127-1638_8736---,00.html. |
| Notary provisions: | Length of commission is for six years (commission expires on notary's birthday after sixth year). |
| | Seal requirements: recommended |
| | Journal requirements: recommended by the state |
| | $10,000 bond required |
| Notary fee guidelines: | Acknowledgments: $10 |
| | Jurats: $10 |
| | Oaths and affirmations $10 |

# Minnesota

| Eligibility requirements: | 18 years of age |
| --- | --- |
| | No minimum residency |
| | Commuting non-residents may apply if they are a resident of a state that borders Minnesota (ex. Iowa, North Dakota, South Dakota, or Wisconsin) |
| **Application process:** | Meet eligibility requirements. |
| | Complete application. |
| | Mail application along with filing fee to secretary of state. |
| | Once application is approved, you must file your commission with your county of residence and pay a recording fee. |
| | For detailed information, visit **https://notary.sos.state.mn.us**. |
| **Notary provisions:** | Length of commission is five years or less. A notary's commission expires on January 31 of the fifth year following the year of issue. |
| | Seal requirements: inked stamp |
| | Journal requirements: recommended |
| | No bond requirement |
| **Notary fee guidelines:** | Acknowledgments: $1 |
| | Jurats: $1 |
| | Oaths and affirmations: $1 |
| | Protests: $1 + $1 for notice with copy |

# Mississippi

| Eligibility requirements: | 18 years of age |
| --- | --- |
| | No minimum residency |
| | Must be a registered voter and pass an exam |
| | State-required notary course must be completed |
| | Must not have a felony conviction |

| Application process: | Meet eligibility requirements. |
|---|---|
| | Complete application form. |
| | Obtain $5,000 bond. |
| | Obtain seal or stamp. |
| | File bond and oath of office with the secretary of state. |
| | Submit application form and fee to the secretary of state. |
| | For detailed information, visit **www.sos.state.ms.us/busserv/notaries/index.asp**. |
| Notary provisions: | Length of commission is four years. |
| | Seal requirements: embosser or ink stamp |
| | Journal requirements: required by law |
| | $5,000 bond requirement |
| Notary fee guidelines: | Acknowledgments: $2 to $5 |
| | Jurats: $2 to $5 |
| | Oaths and affirmations: $2 to $5 |

# Missouri

| Eligibility requirements: | 18 years of age |
|---|---|
| | No minimum residency |
| | Must be able to read and write in English |
| | Must be a registered voter of the county where notary is commissioned or a U.S. resident alien |
| | Must complete state-approved notary course |
| Application process: | Meet eligibility requirements. |
| | Familiarize yourself with the state's notary handbook. |
| | Take a notary training course. |
| | Complete application. |

| | |
|---|---|
| | Submit application form, fee, and proof of course completion to secretary of state. |
| | Purchase your notary bond. |
| | After your commission is issued, appear in person at county clerk's office with bond and take oath before being able to practice as a notary. |
| | For detailed information, visit **www.sos.mo.gov/business/commissions/formspubs.asp**. |
| **Notary provisions:** | Length of commission is four years. |
| | Seal requirements: embosser or black ink stamp |
| | Journal requirements: required by law |
| | $10,000 bond requirement |
| **Notary fee guidelines:** | Acknowledgments: $2 |
| | Jurats: $2 |
| | Oaths and affirmations: $1 |

# Montana

| | |
|---|---|
| **Eligibility requirements:** | 18 years of age |
| | One-year minimum residency |
| | Must be U.S. citizen |
| | No felony convictions |
| **Application process:** | Meet eligibility requirements |
| | Complete application form. |
| | Obtain $10,000 bond. |
| | Take an oath of office and have it notarized as part of your application form. |
| | Submit application form, filing fee, and bond to secretary of state's office. |
| | For detailed information, visit **www.sos.mt.gov/Notary/index.asp**. |

| Notary provisions: | Length of commission is four years. |
|---|---|
| | Seal requirements: embosser or ink stamp |
| | Journal requirements: recommended |
| | $10,000 bond requirement |
| Notary fee guidelines: | Acknowledgments: $5 first signature, $1 for each additional signature |
| | Jurats: $5 |
| | Oaths and affirmations: $5 |

# Nebraska

| Eligibility requirements: | 19 years of age |
|---|---|
| | No minimum residency |
| | No felony convictions |
| | No convictions of crimes related to fraud |
| Application process: | Meet eligibility requirements. |
| | Must pass state-issued notary exam |
| | Obtain $15,000 bond. |
| | After successfully passing exam, complete notary commission application. |
| | Submit application form, commission fee, bond, and confirmation of passing exam to secretary of state's office. |
| | For detailed information, visit **www.sos.state.ne.us/business/notary**. |
| Notary provisions: | Length of commission is four years. |
| | Seal requirements: inked stamp |
| | Journal requirements: recommended by the state |
| | $15,000 bond requirement |

| Notary fee guidelines: | Acknowledgments: $5 |
|---|---|
| | Jurats: $2 |
| | Oaths and affirmations: $2 |
| | Protests: $1 + $2 recording fee and $2 for each notice |

# Nevada

| Eligibility requirements: | 18 years of age |
|---|---|
| | No minimum residency |
| | Must not be convicted of a felony |
| | State-required notary course |
| Application process: | Meet eligibility requirements |
| | Complete mandatory notary training course. |
| | Obtain a bond in the amount of $10,000. |
| | File your bond with the county clerk and take an oath. |
| | The county clerk will then provide you with a filing notice. |
| | Submit application form, filing notice, and application fee to the secretary of state. |
| | For detailed information, visit **http://nvsos.gov/index.aspx?page=165**. |
| Notary provisions: | Length of commission is four years |
| | Seal requirements: inked stamp |
| | Journal requirements: required by state |
| | $10,000 bond requirement |
| Notary fee guidelines: | Acknowledgments: $5 for first signature, $2.50 for each additional signature |
| | Jurats: $5 per signature |
| | Oaths and affirmations; $2.50 |

# New Hampshire

| Eligibility requirements: | 18 years of age |
|---|---|
| | No minimum residency |
| | Must be endorsed by two notaries public and one registered voter of New Hampshire must endorse the application for appointment. |
| Application process: | Meet eligibility requirements. |
| | Complete application form and records check form. |
| | Submit both forms to the secretary of state's office with fee. |
| | After your commission is approved, you will receive via postal mail your commission, oath, index cards, and other information. |
| | Sign and take your oath in the presence of two notary publics or two justices of the peace or one notary public and one justice of the peace. |
| | Return your oath to the secretary of state's office for filing. |
| | Sign index card and return to the superior court of the county in which you reside. |
| | For detailed information, visit **www.sos.nh.gov/notary.html**. |
| Notary provisions: | Length of commission is five years. |
| | Seal requirements: embosser or inked stamp |
| | Journal requirements: recommended by the state |
| | No bond requirement |
| Notary fee guidelines: | Acknowledgments: $10 maximum |
| | Jurats: $10 maximum |
| | Oaths and affirmations: $10 maximum |

# New Jersey

| | |
|---|---|
| **Eligibility requirements:** | 18 years of age |
| | No minimum residency |
| | Must be endorsed by state senator, secretary of state, or assistant secretary |
| | No major convictions |
| **Application process:** | Meet eligibility requirements |
| | Complete application form. |
| | Obtain endorsement from a member of the legislature. |
| | Send application materials along with filing fee to the office of state treasurer. |
| | Once application is approved, applicant must take commission certificate and oath qualification certificate to the county clerk's office for filing. |
| | Applicant takes oath at county clerk's office and pays filing fee. |
| | For detailed information, visit **www.state.nj.us/treasury/ revenue/ dcr/programs/notary.shtml**. |
| **Notary provisions:** | Length of commission is five years. |
| | Seal requirements: recommended |
| | Journal requirements: recommended |
| | No bond requirement |
| **Notary fee guidelines:** | Acknowledgments: $2.50 |
| | Jurats: $1 |
| | Oaths and affirmations: $2.50 |
| | Protests: $2 + $.10 for each notice (plus postage) |

# New Mexico

| Eligibility requirements: | 18 years of age |
|---|---|
| | No minimum residency |
| | Must be endorsed by two residents |
| | Must be fluent in English; must read and write in English |
| | Have never pleaded guilty or been convicted of a felony |
| | Have not had your notary commission revoked in the past five years |
| **Application process:** | Meet eligibility requirements. |
| | Complete application form. |
| | Order stamp or embosser. |
| | Have two state residents endorse you on your application. |
| | Take your oath in the presence of a notary public and have them notarize your application. |
| | Obtain a $10,000 bond. |
| | Return completed application form, bond, and fee to the secretary of state's office. |
| | For detailed information, visit **www.sos.state.nm.us/Main/Operations/Notary-Info.htm.** |
| **Notary provisions:** | Length of commission is four years. |
| | Seal requirements: embosser or inked stamp |
| | Journal requirements: required by law for protests, recommended for other notarizations |
| | $10,000 bond requirement |
| **Notary fee guidelines:** | Acknowledgments: $5 |
| | Jurats: $5 |
| | Oaths and affirmations: $5 |

# New York

| Eligibility requirements: | 18 years of age |
| --- | --- |
| | No minimum residency |
| | Exam is required for non-attorney |
| **Application process:** | Meet eligibility requirements |
| | Complete application form. |
| | Take and successfully pass state-issued notary exam. |
| | Submit application form with fee and pass slip from your exam to secretary of state's office. |
| | For detailed information, visit **www.dos.state.ny.us/lcns/notary1.htm.** |
| **Notary provisions:** | Length of commission is four years. |
| | Seal requirements: recommended |
| | Journal requirements: recommended |
| | No bond requirement |
| **Notary fee guidelines:** | Acknowledgments: $2 + $2 for each sworn witness |
| | Jurats: $2 |
| | Oaths and affirmations: $2 |
| | Protests: $.75 plus $.10 for each notice |

# North Carolina

| Eligibility requirements: | 18 years of age |
| --- | --- |
| | No minimum residency |
| | Must be endorsed by an elected official and notary course instructor |
| | Must complete training course |
| | Signature of applicant must be notarized |
| | Must be able to read, speak, and write in English |

| | |
|---|---|
| | Must pass state exam, unless applicant is already a member of the North Carolina State Bar |
| | Must possess a high school diploma or equivalent |
| **Application process:** | Meet eligibility requirements. |
| | Pass the state-administered notary course. |
| | Complete application form. |
| | Obtain the recommendation of one publicly elected official in the state of North Carolina. |
| | Submit application form, fee, and proof of course completion to secretary of state's office. |
| | For detailed information, visit **www.secretary.state.nc.us/notary**. |
| **Notary provisions:** | Length of commission is five years. |
| | Seal requirements: embosser or inked stamp |
| | Journal requirements: recommended by the state |
| | No bond requirement |
| **Notary fee guidelines:** | Acknowledgments: $5 |
| | Oaths and affirmations: $5 |

# North Dakota

| | |
|---|---|
| **Eligibility requirements:** | 18 years of age |
| | 30-day minimum residency |
| **Application process:** | Meet eligibility requirements. |
| | Complete application form. |
| | Obtain a $7,500 bond. |
| | Submit application form, fee, and proof of bond to secretary of state's office. |
| | Once application is approved, applicant will receive a certificate of authorization. With this certificate, you may now order your stamp/seal. |

| | |
|---|---|
| | Once you receive your stamp/seal, affix an impression of it to the certificate of authorization and return to the secretary of state for filing. |
| | For detailed information, visit **www.nd.gov/sos/notaryserv**. |
| **Notary provisions:** | Length of commission is six years |
| | Seal requirements: embossed or ink stamp; must be clearly reproducible by a photocopy |
| | Journal requirements: recommended by the state |
| | $7,500 bond requirement |
| **Notary fee guidelines:** | Acknowledgments: $5 |
| | Jurats: $5 |
| | Oaths and affirmations: $5 |

# Ohio

| | |
|---|---|
| **Eligibility requirements:** | 18 years of age |
| | 30-day minimum residency |
| | Must be endorsed by a judge |
| | Must pass state exam |
| | Background check |
| **Application process:** | Meet eligibility requirements. |
| | Complete application. |
| | Submit application with fee to the secretary of state's office. |
| | After you are approved, record your commission with the clerk of court of common pleas of the county where you live. |
| | For detailed information, visit **www.sos.state.oh.us/SOS/Notary/NotaryFAQs.aspx**. |

| Notary provisions: | Length of commission is five years. |
|---|---|
| | Seal requirements: embosser or ink stamp |
| | Journal requirements: required for protests, recommended for all other acts |
| | No bond requirement |
| Notary fee guidelines: | Acknowledgments: $2 |
| | Jurats: $1.50 |
| | Oaths and affirmations: $1 |
| | Protests: $1 plus expenses |

# Oklahoma

| Eligibility requirements: | 18 years of age |
|---|---|
| | No minimum residency |
| Application process: | Meet eligibility requirements. |
| | Complete application. |
| | Obtain $1,000 bond. |
| | Submit application form, bond, and fee to the secretary of state. |
| | For detailed information, visit **www.sos.ok.gov/notary/default.aspx**. |
| Notary provisions: | Length of commission is four years. |
| | Seal requirements: embosser or ink stamp |
| | Journal requirements: recommended by the state |
| | $1,000 bond requirement |
| Notary fee guidelines: | Acknowledgments: $5 |
| | Jurats: $5 |
| | Oaths and affirmations: $5 |
| | Protests: $5 |

# Oregon

| Eligibility requirements: | 18 years of age |
| --- | --- |
| | No minimum residency |
| | Must satisfactorily pass exam |
| | Must complete three-hour notary course |
| | No felony convictions |
| **Application process:** | Meet eligibility requirements. |
| | Complete notary course. |
| | Pass an online test. |
| | Complete application; be sure to include the notary education number on your application (you will be provided with this number upon passing your exam. |
| | Submit your application to the secretary of state's office. |
| | You will be sent a certificate of authorization to complete with your stamp. |
| | Submit your stamped certificate to secretary of state. |
| | For detailed information, visit **www.filinginoregon.com/notary**. |
| **Notary provisions:** | Length of commission is four years. |
| | Seal requirements: blank inked stamp |
| | Journal requirements: required by law |
| | No bond requirement |
| **Notary fee guidelines:** | Acknowledgments: $5 |
| | Jurats: $5 |
| | Oaths and affirmations: $1 |
| | Protests: $5 |

# Pennsylvania

| Eligibility requirements: | 18 years of age |
| --- | --- |
| | No minimum residency, but must reside and/or work in the state |
| | Must be endorsed by state senator |
| | Must complete notary education class |
| Application process: | Meet eligibility requirements. |
| | Complete notary course. |
| | Complete application form, including endorsement of the state senator. |
| | Send application along with fee, endorsement of senator, and proof of course completion to the department of state. |
| | Notary must obtain $10,000 bond within 45 days of initial commission, and record bond and oath with prothonotary of the county. |
| | For detailed information, visit **www.dos.state.pa.us/ notaries/cwp/view.asp?a=1240&q=445035**. |
| Notary provisions: | Length of commission is four years. |
| | Seal requirements: inked stamp; embosser optional |
| | Journal requirements: required by law |
| | $10,000 bond requirement |
| Notary fee guidelines: | Acknowledgments: $5 first signature, $2 each additional signature |
| | Jurats: $5 |
| | Oaths and affirmations: $5 |
| | Protests: $3 per page |

\*\*\* Notaries in Pennsylvania are also able to process certain Department of Transportation documents as part of their notary responsibilities. Some of these additional tasks include the processing of titles, registration, and tags. To perform these duties, notaries must register with the Regulated Client Services Section of Penn DOT's Dealer Agent Services Unit (see previous link for further information). \*\*\*

# Rhode Island

| Eligibility requirements: | 18 years of age |
| --- | --- |
| | No minimum residency |
| | Must be endorsed by member of local board of canvassers |
| | Must be a registered voter |
| | Must read and write in English |
| Application process: | Meet eligibility requirements. |
| | Complete application form. |
| | Obtain an endorsement from a member of local board of canvassers. |
| | Submit application form with fee to secretary of state's office. |
| | For detailed information, visit **www.corps.state.ri.us/notaries/notaries.htm**. |
| Notary provisions: | Length of commission is four years. |
| | Seal requirements: recommended |
| | Journal requirements: recommended by the state |
| | No bond requirement |
| Notary fee guidelines: | Acknowledgments $1 |
| | Jurats $.25 |
| | Oaths and affirmations: no fee prescribed |
| | Protests: not to exceed $2 and not to exceed $1.25 for notices |

# South Carolina

| Eligibility requirements: | 18 years of age |
| --- | --- |
| | No minimum residency |
| | Must be endorsed by half of the legislators in county or local senator and representative |
| | Must be a registered voter |

| Application process: | Meet eligibility requirements. |
| --- | --- |
| | Complete application. |
| | Submit application form and fee to secretary of state. |
| | For detailed information, visit **www.scsos.com/Notaries_and_Apostilles**. |
| Notary provisions: | Length of commission is ten years. |
| | Seal requirements: required by law |
| | Journal requirements: recommended by the state |
| | No bond requirement |
| Notary fee guidelines: | Acknowledgments: $.50 |
| | Jurats: $.25 |
| | Oaths and affirmations have no prescribed fees. |
| | Protests: $.50 + postage + $.10/100 words for duplication of certificate + $.50 for attending a person to prove any matter |

**Notaries licensed in the state of South Carolina may perform marriage ceremonies within the boundaries of the state. **

# South Dakota

| Eligibility requirements: | 18 years of age |
| --- | --- |
| | No minimum residency |
| Application process: | Meet eligibility requirements. |
| | Complete application form. |
| | Purchase a notary seal or stamp. |
| | Purchase a $5,000 bond. |
| | Submit completed application with proof of bond and application fee to the secretary of state. |
| | For detailed information, visit **www.sdsos.gov/adminservices/notaries.shtm**. |

| Notary provisions: | Length of commission is six years. |
| --- | --- |
| | Seal requirements: embosser or inked stamp |
| | Journal requirements: recommended by the state |
| | $5,000 bond requirement |
| Notary fee guidelines: | Acknowledgments $10 |
| | Jurats $10 |
| | Oaths and affirmations $10 |

# Tennessee

| Eligibility requirements: | 18 years of age |
| --- | --- |
| | No minimum residency |
| | Must be endorsed by county commissioner |
| | Must be approved by vote of county legislative body |
| Application process: | Meet eligibility requirements. |
| | Complete application form. |
| | Obtain endorsement of county commissioner. |
| | Submit application fee and form to the secretary of state. |
| | Once application is approved, obtain a $10,000 bond. |
| | Submit bond and take oath with county clerk. |
| | For detailed information, visit **www.tennessee.gov/sos/bus_svc/notary.htm**. |
| Notary provisions: | Length of commission is four years. |
| | Seal requirements: embosser or inked stamp |
| | Journal requirements: required by law |
| | $10,000 bond requirement |
| Notary fee guidelines: | Acknowledgments $2.25 |
| | Jurats $2.25 |
| | Oaths and affirmations $2.25 |
| | Protests $1.50 + $1 for recording |

# Texas

| Eligibility requirements: | 18 years of age |
|---|---|
| | No minimum residency, but must be a resident of Texas |
| | No felony convictions |
| Application process: | Meet eligibility requirements. |
| | Complete application form. |
| | Obtain a $10,000 bond. |
| | Submit application form, bond, and fee to secretary of state. |
| | For detailed information, visit **www.sos.state.tx.us/statdoc/index.shtml**. |
| Notary provisions: | Length of commission is four years. |
| | Seal requirements: embosser or inked stamp (must be reproducible by photocopy) |
| | Journal requirements: required by law |
| | $10,000 bond requirement |
| Notary fee guidelines: | Acknowledgments: $6 for first signature, $1 for each additional signature |
| | Jurats: $6 |
| | Oaths and affirmations: $6 |
| | Protests: $4 + $4 for certificate + $1 for each notice |

# Utah

| Eligibility requirements: | 18 years of age |
|---|---|
| | 30-day minimum residency |
| | Must be endorsed by two Utah residents over 18 years of age |
| | Must pass the exam with 31 questions answered correctly out of 35 |
| | Must be able to read and write in English |
| | Must be a resident of Utah or a legal alien |

| Application process: | Meet eligibility requirements. |
| --- | --- |
| | Take state-issued notary exam. |
| | Complete application form. |
| | After you are notified that you have passed your exam, obtain a $5,000 bond. |
| | Submit application form, fee, bond, test score result, and either a copy of your birth certificate, U.S. passport, or green card to the State of Utah. |
| | Once your application is processed, you will receive a Certificate of Authority of Notary Public. |
| | Order your notary stamp. |
| | For detailed information, visit **http://notary.utah.gov**. |
| Notary provisions: | Length of commission is four years. |
| | Seal requirements: inked stamp |
| | Journal requirements: recommended by the state |
| | $5,000 bond requirement |
| Notary fee guidelines: | Acknowledgments: $5 |
| | Jurats: $5 |
| | Oaths and affirmations: $5 |

# Vermont

| Eligibility requirements: | 18 years of age |
| --- | --- |
| | No minimum residency |
| Application process: | Meet eligibility requirements. |
| | Complete an application form. |
| | Take an oath in the presence of a notary public. |
| | Submit your application form and fee to your county clerk's office. |
| | For detailed information, visit **http://vermont-archives.org/notary/index.htm**. |

| Notary provisions: | Length of commission is up to four years based on date commissioned. All Vermont notaries' commissions expire on February 10 every four years. |
| --- | --- |
| | Seal requirements: recommended |
| | Journal requirements: recommended |
| | No bond required |
| Notary fee guidelines: | Acknowledgments: $.50 |
| | Jurats: $.50 |
| | Oaths and affirmations: $.50 |
| | Protests: $2, including notices |

# Virginia

| Eligibility requirements: | 18 years of age |
| --- | --- |
| | No minimum residency |
| | A notary public must be endorsed by a clerk, attorney of the commonwealth, a member of the Virginia General Assembly. |
| | No felony convictions, unless pardoned |
| Application process: | Meet eligibility requirements. |
| | Complete application form. |
| | Obtain an endorsement from clerk or deputy clerk of any general/district court or an attorney/assistant attorney of the commonwealth or attorney general or assistant attorney general or a member of the Virginia General Assembly. |
| | Submit application form and fee to treasurer of Virginia; |
| | Within 60 days of commission, new notary must go to a local court of their choice to take their oath. |
| | For detailed information, visit **www.commonwealth.virginia.gov/OfficialDocuments/Notary/notary.cfm**. |

| | |
|---|---|
| **Notary provisions:** | Length of commission is four years. |
| | Seal requirements: required |
| | Journal requirements: recommended by the state |
| | No bond requirement |
| **Notary fee guidelines:** | Acknowledgments: $5 |
| | Jurats: $5 |
| | Oaths and affirmations: $5 |

# Washington

| | |
|---|---|
| **Eligibility requirements:** | 18 years of age |
| | No minimum residency |
| | Must be endorsed by three unrelated adult residents of the state who are also registered voters |
| | Must be able to read and write in English |
| **Application process:** | Meet eligibility requirements. |
| | Complete application form. |
| | Obtain $10,000 bond. |
| | Submit application form with fee and bond to secretary of state. |
| | For detailed information, visit **www.dol.wa.gov/business/notary**. |
| **Notary provisions:** | Length of commission is four years. |
| | Seal requirements: embosser or inked stamp |
| | Journal requirements: recommended by the state |
| | $10,000 bond requirement |
| **Notary fee guidelines:** | Acknowledgments $10 for each signature |
| | Jurats: $10 |
| | Oaths and affirmations: $10 |
| | Protests: $10 + $10 for being present at demand, tender, or deposit |

# West Virginia

| | |
|---|---|
| **Eligibility requirements:** | 18 years of age |
| | 30-day minimum residency |
| | Must be endorsed by three qualified electors |
| | Must be able to read and write in English |
| **Application process:** | Meet eligibility requirements. |
| | Complete application. |
| | Obtain three character witnesses. |
| | Submit application form and fee to secretary of state. |
| | Once your application is approved, you will receive via postal mail your commission certificate and notary stamp card. |
| | Order your rubber stamp seal. |
| | Imprint your notary stamp on card and return to secretary of state for filing. |
| | For detailed information, visit **www.wvsos.com/notary/main.htm**. |
| **Notary provisions:** | Length of commission is ten years. |
| | Seal requirements: inked stamp |
| | Journal requirements: recommended by the state |
| | No bond requirement |
| **Notary fee guidelines:** | Acknowledgments: $2 |
| | Jurats: $2 |
| | Oaths and affirmations: $2 |
| | |

# Wisconsin

| | |
|---|---|
| **Eligibility requirements:** | 18 years of age |
| | No minimum residency |
| | Must have at least an eighth-grade education |
| | No convictions related to notarial acts |
| **Application process:** | Meet eligibility requirements. |
| | Complete application form. |
| | Complete bond/oath form. |
| | Submit forms and application fee to secretary of state. |
| | For detailed information, visit **www.sos.state.wi.us/notary.htm**. |
| **Notary provisions:** | Length of commission is four years. |
| | Seal requirements: embosser or inked stamp |
| | Journal requirements: recommended by the state |
| | $500 bond requirement |
| **Notary fee guidelines:** | Acknowledgments: $.50 |
| | Jurats: no prescribed fee |
| | Oaths and affirmations: no prescribed fee |
| | Protests: $1 + $.50 for copy + $.50 for each notice |
| | |

# Wyoming

| | |
|---|---|
| **Eligibility requirements:** | 18 years of age |
| | No minimum residency |
| | Must be able to read and write in English |
| | Exam is encouraged, though not mandatory |
| **Application process:** | Meet eligibility requirements. |
| | Study the notary handbook. |
| | Take notary exam (it is encouraged, though not required). |

| | |
|---|---|
| | Submit application form, fee, and test (if applicable) to the secretary of state. |
| | Obtain a $500 bond. |
| | File bond within 60 days of your commission with your county clerk. |
| | For detailed information, visit **http://soswy.state.wy.us/default.aspx**. |
| **Notary provisions:** | Length of commission is four years. |
| | Seal requirements: embosser or inked stamp |
| | Journal requirements: recommended by the state |
| | $500 bond requirement |
| **Notary fee guidelines:** | Acknowledgments: $2 |
| | Jurats: $2 |
| | Oaths and affirmations: $2 |
| | Protests: $2 |

A P P E N D I X   C :

# Notary Web Site Resources

The following are Notary Associations:

## National Notary Association

Website: **www.nationalnotary.org**

Phone: 800-US NOTARY

National Headquarters:

9350 De Soto Avenue, P.O. Box 2402

Chatsworth, CA 91311-2402

## The American Society of Notaries

Website: **http://notaries.org**

Phone: 850-671-5164

P.O. Box 5707

Tallahassee, FL 32314

## North American Notary Association

Website: **http://nanotary.com**

Phone: 877-815-8774

450 Fletcher Parkway, Suite 219

El Cajon, CA 92020

The following are resources for the small business owner:

U.S. Small Business Administration

**www.sba.gov**

Entrepreneur

**www.entrepreneur.com**

About.com: Small Business Information

**http://sbinformation.about.com**

IRS: Small Business Information

**www.irs.gov/businesses/small**

BusinessWeek: Small Business Information

**www.businessweek.com/smallbiz**

Small Business Resources for Women

**www.womanowned.com**

National Women's Business Council

**www.womenbiz.gov**

Business Licenses

**www.usa.gov**

# APPENDIX D:
# Sample Business Plan

## Sample Business Plan

9/9/09

Prepared by:
Mick Spillane

Acme Notary Services, LLC
Noah Fence, Certified Notary Public and President

LeRoy, NY 14482

555-555-5555

acmenotary@gmail.com

# Table of Contents

# Executive Summary

Acme Notary Services, LLC (ANS) is a startup company in the western New York area. The mission of ANS is to provide much-needed notary and real estate services in the greater Rochester and Buffalo areas. ANS is a full-service mobile notary service, providing virtual bankruptcy assistance, signing services, and wedding services.

# Work Experience

Mr. Fence's work experience has been as follows:

1995 – 1998 Position _____ at _____ Co. Describe your work responsibilities in detail: _____

1998 – 2006 Product manager at Modern Transitor Co. Describe your work responsibilities in detail: _____

I have included a list of work references and character references as Exhibit A.

I have personal contacts in _____ who are ready to employ my services.

# Education

Mr. Fence's education includes: _____ grade school, graduation from _____ high school (class of _____).

My higher education includes a _____ degree earned in _____ at _____, _____ year.

In _____ school I participated in the following activities: _____.
I have also taken the following courses and seminars: _____, _____, and _____.

My hobbies are: _____

My ongoing education includes subscriptions to the following professional journals and industry trade periodicals: _____.

# Consultants

ANS knows the importance of having professional advisers in place before starting a business. The following is a list of my professional advisers:

Attorney: Karen Katchum

Accountant: Nico Numbers

Insurance agent: Pete Premium

Banker: Devon Q. Deeppockets

E-Commerce consultant: Mary Smith

Other: _____

Other: _____

# Licenses

Acme Notary Services will require the following licenses. I will need to research the requirements for my own location and circumstances:

County and state offices: This could include the business license department, planning department, building department, health department, et cetera.

Norman Numbers, my accountant, will give me advice on federal, state, and local reporting and licensing requirements.

# Insurance

ANS plans to use the services of Pete Premium as its insurance agent. ANS insurance policies and limits of coverage are as follows:

Mr. Premium will provide me with a tabulation of all insurance policies and limits of E & O insurance.

# The Business

ANS will be a limited liability partnership registered in the state of New York for tax purposes. Its founder is Mr. Noah Fence, a notary signing agent for Heidegger's Notary Services Company, where he worked for 25 years.

The company's main clients will be banks, credit unions, mortgage companies, title, escrow, closing, and signing companies. The company will also serve anyone else in the public seeking a notary service. Because Mr. Fence falls into this demographic group and knows and understands this market's needs, he believes that he can appeal to such clients far more than most other competitors can.

# Business Concept

ANS offers comprehensive notary, mortgage, and title services to a diverse set of clients. ANS will have a dominant position as the premier notary services company in western New York. In addition, ANS will offer the following a full range of services to fulfill all client needs:

- Mobile notary services
- Loan document signing
- Real estate closings
- Wills, weddings, power of attorney, and child custody
- Title transfer

- ▶ Service for the legal profession
- ▶ Title and mortgage services

# Business Organization

ANS plans to form a _____ for a business. It is Mr. Fence's intention to grow Acme Notary Services into a large firm with national relationships. The initial and ongoing costs of operating as a _____ will be a necessary business expense. Also, because a properly run _____ will afford ANS some limits of liability, I feel this is the right form of business for me. I intend to depend on my attorney to handle all aspects of setting up the _____ and maintaining proper _____ records.

The following is an itemized cost-breakdown of the services of Acme Notary Services that will be the initial line. The initial target mark-up will be _____%.

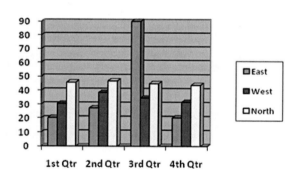

# Financial Strategy

ANS requirements for startup capital are as follows:

See Appendix B for a description of items for which ANS will require either startup capital or financing. These items include supplies, a computer, equipment and fixtures, tooling, travel expenses, and startup overhead expenses. These expenses are included in my monthly cash-flow projection to indicate the ongoing requirements for cash.

Although I will not depend on banks for financing, there will be other resources available to me, such as leasing of equipment and fixtures, credit from suppliers, mortgage financing, et cetera. ANS referrals include the following helpful contacts to lending institutions: my accountant, the Small Business Administration, friends, relatives, et cetera.

ANS is prepared to make presentations to potential lenders. My presentation kit includes this business plan, my personal financial statement, and personal tax returns. I will be prepared to be specific in my needs for financing, the payback program, and my sources of repayment. I will furnish potential lenders a cash-flow projection showing sources of repayments, and I will be conservative in my forecasts.

# Objectives

Establish and maintain close contacts with residential real estate listing services, law offices, and all other service organizations that ANS uses, such as Paddy O'Toole's Mortgage Service Company.

Keep close contact with clients and establish long-term relationships with these clients to produce repeat business and attain a superior reputation.

Establish a complete service experience for our clients that include the following: e-signings, trust agreements, business partnerships and contracts, divorce agreements, et cetera.

# The Market

ANS will be working for banks, credit unions, mortgage companies, title and escrow companies, closing companies, and signing companies, as well as targeting the public that may require my services.

# Market Analysis

ANS plans to keep the required startup expenses and funding modest. They include expenses and cash needed to support operations until revenues reach an acceptable level. I will not initially benefit from pricing power in marketing my ANS services. Individual customers will be primarily interested in price. In order to attain lower costs than my larger competitors, ANS plans to do the following: _____.

ANS's definitive goal is to construct a notary service so exceptional and promote it so effectively that consumers will be willing to pay a premium. The long-term objective is to build a market that is not entirely based on price. Specific unique features will include the following: _____.

The liabilities for ANS will come from outside private investors and management investment; ANS is currently borrowing from Banco Popular, with the principal to be paid off in three years.

The company expects to reach profitability within two years and does not anticipate any problems with cash flow. ANS conservatively believes that, during the first three years, average profitability per month will be adequate.

# The Competition

ANS's principal competitor is the Notary Hut. Included are a list of all major competitors in this business and a brief sketch, including their customers. (Provide a tabulation of these competitors).

# Competition's Weak Points

The Notary Hut, which has a 15-year history of success, has gained strong brand recognition, but it has developed a large overhead structure, which ANS will not have. They are slow to make changes to modern technologies and marketing. ANS plans to overcome their leadership with fresh new designs, artwork, and attractive price packaging to be competitive. I intend to introduce additions and refinements to my services continually.

ANS's end-user profile is for younger clients who are not impressed by old-line brand names. Operating with a very low overhead, I believe I can gain a foothold in this market. A similar profile of my other principal competitors, indicating their weak spots and how I plan to capitalize on these deficiencies, is enclosed.

# Marketing Plan

ANS plans to focus all preliminary marketing efforts on establishing the groundwork in the western New York market area. I will personally be responsible for the contacts with the appropriate clients and institutions.

# Internet Marketing and Advertising

A website focusing on Acme Notary Services will be an important tool in my overall marketing program. I plan to build and install www.nfnotary.com, which I have already registered. This will permit my discounts to certain institutions and customers to have access to my virtual services via my website. I plan to hire Mary Smith of Smith E-Commerce Consulting Company to design, install, and maintain this site.

The features of the **www.acmenotary.com** site will include the following:

▶ Excellent user-friendly navigational features and prompt loading

▶ The site will provide useful content including detailed information about all my services.

▶ Steps for retaining my services will be designed and implemented.

▶ I intend to use the site to generate client feedback to help improve every aspect of my service, operation, and business procedures.

# Budget for Internet Advertising

The budget for design, implementation, and startup of the e-commerce site will be _____. This is based on a firm contract with Mary Smith of Smith E-Commerce Consulting Company. The estimated monthly maintenance cost to support the site will be $_____.

# Advertising

Short-range plan (6 to 12 months): Initially, my advertising and promotion will be done on an entirely personal basis without any budget for paid advertising. My clients require services in person. My plan is to limit my advertising budget to personal travel expenses in making these presentations and follow-up presentations.

Mid-range plan (12 to 36 months): To establish brand recognition on a national level, I plan to budget _____% of my sales to joint advertising with my discount department store customers. I will solicit presentations from local advertising agencies.

Long-range plan: I plan to build brand recognition and loyalty aggressively by budgeting _____% of sales, which will be allocated between space advertising in trade journals, appropriate business magazines, and joint advertising with my customers.

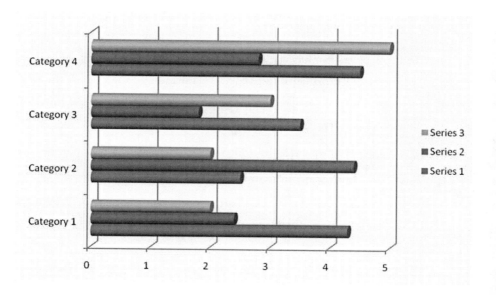

# Strategies and Vision

ANS has a long-term plan to use the specialized business knowledge that Mr. Fence has gained. The business relationships Mr. Fence has acquired include banks, credit unions, mortgage companies, title and escrow, closing companies, and signing companies. They are: _____, _____, _____. (List and explain in detail how they will help you).

The reasons that Mr. Fence feels plans are realistic are the following: _____ _____.

There are special market conditions that are favorable to ANS getting started at this time.

They are as follows: _____.

# Criteria of Location

During the ANS start-up phase of approximately six to 12 months, Mr. Fence plans to work out of his home office. Once the business is established, the ANS initial office requirements will be approximately 1,000 square feet with two private offices and a secretarial area. The office criteria will include:

▸ Convenience to home

▸ A short-term lease of one to two years with two one-year options

▸ A lease provision that the landlord provide me expansion space as required with an option to terminate without penalty clause if expansion space is not available

▸ Office layout, including tenant improvements provided by the landlord

▸ Lawyer review of the lease

▸ Use of the lease check-off list that is attached as an exhibit

The use of these location criteria will provide ANS with the experience in handling larger leases for space in the relatively near future. ANS will be incurring large lease obligations that will be carefully reviewed. Location studies will include the following:

▸ Space requirements

▸ Future requirements

▸ Site analysis study if needed (attach)

▸ Demographic study if needed (attach)

▸ Lease check-off list (attach)

▸ Estimated occupancy cost as a percent of sales

▸ Zoning and use approvals

# Accounting

Mr. Fence's knowledge of accounting is: _____. (If you are deficient in basic accounting knowledge, then state how you intend to gain this needed know-how.)

My accountant: ANS will work with Norman Numbers.

Accounting software programs: I will be using the following systems: _____ _____.

Method of accounting: I will use the _____ method of accounting.

Business records: I will keep Acme Notary Services accounts and records separate from my personal records.

Tax issues: My accountant, Mr. Numbers, will help me set up records for payments of Social Security tax, estimated income tax payments, payroll taxes and state withholding and sales taxes. My employer identification number (FEIN) is: _____.

Internal controls: Mr. Numbers will also help me set appropriate controls for handling funds in my business, including inventory policy and controls. Purchasing, capital acquisitions, and signing of checks will not be delegated.

Quarterly returns: Taxes will be paid in the appropriate time frames.

Bank account reconciliation: Bank accounts will be reconciled on a monthly basis.

Balance sheet: Attached is a separate exhibit of my starting balance sheet. Included is a schedule of needed equipment and fixtures that will appear on my balance sheet.

Income statements: Attached are my projected income statements for the first six months and one year.

# Cash-Flow Summary

Attached is an exhibit of my one-year cash-flow analysis, including estimated sales, all costs, and capital requirements. I have included a checklist of all expense items for input into my cash flow projections.

# Growth Strategy

ANS will not set an inflexible timetable for expansion, but will wait until a sound basis of experience, earnings, and cash flow is achieved.

Accounting and cash flow controls will be in place with profit and loss statements prepared for individual expansion units on a _____ (monthly, etc) basis.

Internal controls for accounting, money handling, and inventory will be in place.

My attorney will review all documentation regarding expansion. This will include leases, employment and incentive agreements, licensing and franchise agreements, important commitments with vendors and customers, et cetera.

Hiring and training policies will be in place. Fringe benefit plans will be in place.

My intention is to delegate authority and responsibility to expansion management personnel with the following conditions in place:

Managers will be motivated by a profit incentive plan that will be tied to a manager's individual success. My plan will be in writing, simply stated, and will call for frequent periods of accountability. A sample of my manager's incentive compensation plan is attached.

Capital allocations and signing checks will not be delegated.

ANS intends to maintain an ongoing study of my competitors. Their successes and failures will help form guidelines on what to do and not to do.

# Overcoming Obstacles

The ANS policy in handling problems will be to identify and acknowledge issues promptly and honestly. I plan to put the following policies into effect promptly if the following adverse scenarios emerge during my growth program:

The risk of running out of cash: ANS plans to maintain very frequent (_____ monthly?) cash-flow projections. Forecasts for income, expenses, and unanticipated contingencies will be stated conservatively. Any periods of cash deficits will be remedied promptly by cutting costs to maintain a positive cash flow and profitability.

A drop in sales or insufficient sales:

ANS will be prepared to take prompt remedial steps by cutting costs.

ANS will improve every aspect of product value, performance, and image.

ANS will seek out new ways to expand sales by _____.

ANS plan to stick with this specialized business that I know best unless fatally defective.

Dishonesty, theft, and shrinkage: ANS intends to implement the same policies that have been proven by _____ company, one of my biggest competitors.

Business recessions: ANS is prepared to promptly cut costs to maintain liquidity. ANS will also be on the lookout for good business opportunities during periods of adversity.

# Appendix A Communications Tools

ANS plans to use all the computer and communications tools currently available to establish myself on the same level playing field as my large competitors. The following are the tentative specifications and budget for this equipment.

## Resource Requirements:

Notary tools and supplies

Communications

Telephones

Pagers

Facsimile

Computers and software

Internet

## Appendix B

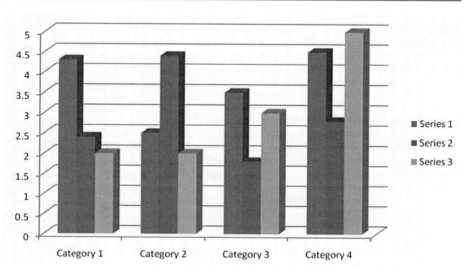

# Bibliography

All Business. "Cash vs. accrual accounting methods." **www.allbusiness.com/accounting-reporting/methods-standards-cash/1308-1.html**

Bargaineering. "What it means to be bonded, licensed & insured." October 30, 2007. **www.bargaineering.com/articles/what-it-means-to-be-bondedlicensed-insured.html**

Duran, Linda M. *Real Estate Loan Signing: Notary Field Manual.* Denver, Colorado: Outskirts Press, 2005.

Harper, Stephen C. *The McGraw-Hill Guide to Starting Your Own Business: A Step-by-Step Blueprint for the First-Time Entrepreneur,* 2nd Edition. New York: McGraw-Hill, 2003.

NotaryTrainer.com. *Notary Public Journal.* South Amboy, New Jersey: Jordania Legal Publishers, LLC, 2006.

Paulson, Edward. *The Complete Idiot's Guide to Starting Your Own Business*, 5th Ed. New York: Alpha Books, 2007.

Pierre-Fleurimond, Gerrie. *Glossary Terms for Title Closers and Mortgage Notaries*. South Amboy, New Jersey: Jordania Legal Publishers, LLC, 2006.

Ready, N.P. *Brooke's Notary*. Great Britain: Sweet & Maxwell Limited, 2002.

Ring, Victoria. *How to Start, Operate and Market a Freelance Notary Signing Agent Business*, 5th Ed. Columbus, Ohio: Graphico Publishing, 2007.

World Intellectual Property Organization. "What is intellectual property?" **www.wipo.int/about-ip/en**

# Author Biographies

A copywriter and marketing consultant, Kristie Lorette is passionate about helping entrepreneurs and businesses create copy and marketing pieces that sizzle, motivate, and sell. It is through her more than 14 years of experience working in various roles of marketing, financial services, real estate, and event planning where Lorette developed her widespread expertise in advanced business and marketing strategies and communications. Lorette earned a B.S. in marketing and a B.S. in multinational business from Florida State University and her M.B.A. from Nova Southeastern University.

Mick Spillane is freelance academic book editor and writer. He has a master's degree in philosophy from The New School for Social Research, where he received a President's Scholarship and a writing award from the Democracy and Cultural Pluralism Foundation. His previous writings include short stories and essays. He resides in Rochester, NY.

# Index